Crossing the boundary

WHAT WILL WOMEN PRIESTS MEAN?

EDITED BY
SUE WALROND-SKINNER

MOWBRAY

262.14342
CRO

In honour of all those women
for whom this moment has come too late
for their own priestly vocation —
especially for Diana and for Frances

Mowbray
A Cassell imprint
Villiers House
41/47 Strand
London
WC2N 5JE

387 Park Avenue South
New York
NY 10016–8810

First published 1994

British Library Cataloguing-in-Publication Data
A catalogue record for this book is available from the
British Library.

ISBN 0–264–67360–3

Phototypeset by Intype, London
Printed and bound in Great Britain by
Biddles Ltd, Guildford and King's Lynn

Contents

Contributors

CHRISTINE FARRINGTON is a priest, co-director of ordinands in the diocese of Ely and canon of Ely Cathedral.

MONICA FURLONG is a writer and biographer, and a former Moderator of the Movement for the Ordination of Women.

JACKIE HAWKINS is a Roman Catholic lay woman and is executive editor of *The Way*.

CLARE HERBERT is a priest and is pastoral care adviser in the lay ministry department in the diocese of London.

UNA KROLL is a contemplative nun, living alone in Monmouth, where she is a deacon in the local parish church.

CATHY MILFORD is a priest and Moderator of the Movement for the Ordination of Women, and adult education adviser in the diocese of Winchester.

MAGGIE ROSS is an Anglican solitary.

JANE SINCLAIR is a priest, residentiary canon and precentor of Sheffield Cathedral, and a member of the Liturgical Commission of the Church of England.

SUE WALROND-SKINNER is a priest, a family therapist and adviser in pastoral care and counselling in the diocese of Southwark.

JANE WILLIAMS is a lay woman, theologian and writer in the Church in Wales.

I

So far in this world

SUE WALROND-SKINNER

As we struggle from our different perceptions to interpret the significance of the ordination of women to the priesthood in the Church of England in 1994, one certainty eclipses all others. The knowledge that this *is* a moment of historical significance— that the moment is *now* and that the moment must not be somehow missed even if it cannot fully be understood. This is the impetus that lies behind the publication of this book of essays. They have been written to honour the moment; to mark it and to try perhaps to understand its significance a little better.

But *what* exactly does this moment mark? Certainly nothing very new in the ways and means of women's ministry in the Church. Apart from the 'ABC' of priesthood, women, both lay and ordained, have already developed a rich variety of ministries, roles and tasks within the Church of England, from running parishes to teaching theology in universities and colleges, to holding senior positions in dioceses, cathedrals and major Christian organizations. It certainly does not mark the priesting of Anglican women for the first time—a fact brought home by the happy coincidence this year of the fiftieth anniversary of the priesting of Li Tim Oi, the first of many women to receive priestly orders as Anglicans. Nor does our priesting this year mark a moment of obvious progress to the vast majority of women in the world who do not belong to any faith community. More significant by far will have been the launch in January 1994 of the campaign Zero Tolerance, to raise public awareness of domestic violence and the way in which the police and the

law must offer more help to the 100,000 women in Britain alone
who each year seek treatment for injuries received in the home
from men. More significant by far will have been the judgement
made in favour of Lorena Bobbitt in the United States who, in
a last effort to end the years of agony and abuse at the hands of
her husband, cut off his penis. The shock waves created by both
the action and the judgement in this case focused with horrific
clarity the ultimate consequences of humanity's inability to con-
tain or manage the opposing differences of gender.

The abused Muslim women of the Balkan states, the homeless
women of Britain, the exploited rural working women in the
fields of southern Asia, the frightened resigned women of
the South African townships, all have more on their minds
at the moment than our priesting.

For many people outside, the Church's obsessional preoccupation with this issue over the last few years, in so far as they
have been aware of the Church at all, must have encouraged
them in their belief that the Church is full of sound and fury,
ultimately signifying nothing that is of importance to their lives.
Yet running through all the accounts of the struggle there has
been a consistent theme, that this moment when it came would
have meaning mainly for those who *did not* belong to the English
church. The articulation of this meaning has sometimes been in
grandiose terms: 'the healing of humanity's basic split' or 'a
symbol of hope for all other women oppressed by the structures
of society'. Sometimes it has been only a whisper. But always
the thought and the hope that the struggle was on behalf of
something *beyond* the theology, the politics and the personnel
of the Church of England.

It is hard to arrive at quite what this meaning might be or to
understand the consequences of our priesting for others. But
hundreds of women deacons have had experiences like the following. On my way to take part in a memorial service for a friend's
mother, I was (unusually) walking through London in my black
shirt and dog collar. Two young men dressed joyfully in leather
and earrings and swinging their beer cans and chips had crossed
over the road. They overtook me and then doubled back in
astonishment.

'You a priest then?'

'No, but maybe I will be soon.'

'Wow. Congratulations then.' (Grabbing me by the hand) 'It's an honour to meet you!'

I looked blank and amazed, but they didn't notice and were soon out of sight, leaving me pondering the oddness of the encounter.

What on earth did I represent to these two young men who seemed to exist in some other world than the one I felt I inhabited? Something that transcended the obvious barriers that lay between us and which would more usually have invited an insult. Something, too, that felt important enough for them to make a huge and spontaneous gesture of connection. Something that spoke to them of hope, perhaps, if only because of its new and different image. And out of that speaking, came the realization for me that part of the meaning of this moment is the possibility and the hope of a newly honed *unity*. A *great* puzzle and a paradox, because the more immediate *disunity* around us feels so very painful. But becoming clearer—though not clear yet—is something of the great uniting meaning of what our priesting may envisage for women and men who come from very many different places.

*

During the period between 11 November 1992 and the first ordinations that took taking place during the spring and summer of 1994, there was a profound silence. Much activity, much re-grouping, yes, but also an emptiness, a paralysis to which several of the contributors to this book draw attention. In Monica's arresting metaphor (Chapter 2) it is as though the Church of England has been having a nervous breakdown. It is an image to which I will return. The vote in favour of the priesthood was in fact a profound shock. It was a shock to those who had struggled so hard to achieve it. It was a shock to those who had struggled so hard to prevent it. It was a shock to bishops and legislators alike. But, most of all, it was a shock to the *organism as a whole*—to the Body in all its interconnected wholeness and in its own vibrant being.

Symbolism, imagery, liturgical expression of fundamental

belief, the role relationships of women and men, clergy and lay, all have been subject to a major psychic upheaval as a result of the ordination of women. Enormous possibilities for growth lie ahead, but, for the moment, the experience of the Church is more like that of a nervous breakdown. The Church as a system is experiencing a profound sense of disequilibrium. This collective organismic experience must continue to be endured and travelled through if the breakdown is to become a breakthrough. But systems in disequilibrium need ways and means of stabilizing themselves. The danger is always that a new pseudo stability is achieved by means of some individuals or groups within the organization being identified as 'the problem', thus relieving others of understanding and working through the meaning of the change process for the Church as a whole.

We are now in a position to look back and reflect a little on how this is being worked out. During the past two years we have seen various groups so identified—women themselves, the opponents, the 'defectors', the bishops, the Synod—all have become 'the problem' in turn, as alliances and groupings have been made and remade. Often other issues and difficulties have coalesced around these divisions. The formation of the group 'Reform' is an example, scapegoating and being scapegoated in its turn, in a kind of interlocking pathological process which reflects the reciprocal and interrelated nature of the unconscious processes going on within the organization. Some of the more disturbing aspects of this interlocking pathology, buried deep in the relationship of the priest and his flock, relate to the way in which the pathological dependency of the one has served to maintain the pathological narcissism of the other. This has, in some quarters of the Church, been a 'family secret', the exposure of which has been deeply feared. The protection of this secret is severely threatened by the advent of women priests and continues to drive the desperate effort on the part of some of the splinter groups to ward off the feared disaster.

The perceptions of each group of itself have also been radically altered by the group's perceptions of others. This has led sometimes to new realignments (amongst Evangelicals, for example, as a result of Reform, and between Evangelicals and others). Sometimes it has led to paralysis or retreat. Thus, bishops sometimes appeared passive and disabled in knowing how to exercise their role as they tried to respond to women's conflicting perceptions of the process and purpose of discerning their priestly vocation. Opponents of the measure have tended to respond by fight or flight. Many have become isolated and depressed. Each grouping has been encouraged to express 'more of the same' defensive strategy in response to the defensive positions of others. Those opponents who are remaining as Anglicans appear to have progressively narrowed the scope of their participation in the Church in a retreat behind a detailed and restricted code of behaviour. Some women have found that the confusion and hostility around them has activated their own aggressive or depressive response. Others have experienced anxiety and fear at the loss of their dependency and yet have felt unable to express their needs very fully when they are supposed now to have 'got what they wanted'.

It is crucially important that we try to attend, and go on attending, to the *process* of all that is taking place within the organism as a whole, in a continuous way, so that the dysfunctional, defensive pressure to act out the confusion and pain is reduced, and the possibility of experiencing new creative growth from this wholly new situation becomes more real. We *have* to come to understand what is now for ever past and what new mysterious truths are on offer waiting to be revealed. We *have* to engage with *the real* and *the now* and with the *new thing* that God has brought into being. And that holds losses and gains in different measure for *all of us*, whatever our views about the ordination of women and whether we are prepared to recognize this ambiguity or not.

The experience for the Church as living organism has been so complex that it is not at all strange that there was such a muted, sombre, uncertain response to the General Synod's vote on 11 November 1992. Nor was there any obvious sense in which the vote marked the end of the struggle. The passage towards the first ordinations was no less fraught with difficulty, even though there was a significant shift of focus. The very knowledge that the major hurdle of that Synod vote had been cleared only served to throw into stark relief new and unexpected difficulties. As Cathy observes in Chapter 4, the testing of the Synod's right in

Church
Council

the courts to make the decision at all; the passage of the legislation through Parliament; the painful necessities of the Act of
Synod; the last-ditch challenge to the Synod's authority, the day
before the measure was finally promulged; the many and various
ways in which the process of discernment of women's vocations
was handled in the dioceses up and down the country; the
arrangements and planning of the ordinations themselves—all of
these matters provided a series of lesser challenges, with their
own anxious and painful moments.

These external factors were partly handled in ways that were
reactive to the sense of psychic shock experienced on 11 November. But they also contributed to and interacted with the difficulties experienced in the interior world of the organism's emotions
and spirit. The aftermath of the shock and the numbed silence
which followed made it particularly difficult for those women
who are most personally affected by the vote to grasp or face up
to their identity as womanly priests. It is not only the lack of
role models, or the taboos of centuries, that have to be loosened
and let go; it is the fact that there have been few people who
have been prepared to hold up a mirror to women, so that
each woman could see herself for who she really is. This process of mirroring is, however, a vital part of each person's
development, from the early mirroring of the baby's identity
by mother to later moments of 'recognition', holding and
reflection of our core identity, offered to us by those who love
us most.

This mirror of recognition has been found by some women in
very unexpected places—like the two young men who mirrored
back to me something of profound importance during our twenty
seconds of encounter. It is the mirror that allows each person to
recognize herself and become who she is.

But for many of us this discovery of ourselves as priests-to-be
has been an uncertain, halting process. For the shocking icono-
clasm of 11 November faced women, already ordained as deacons,
with the personal need to confront the meaning of that decision
for themselves for the first time. Like Christine (Chapter 5) who
has been influenced in her own journey by the opportunities and
privilege of hearing women talk about their unfolding understanding of priesthood, I have had, in a different way, the

privilege of listening to women, individually and in groups, reflect on their struggles and dilemmas, their uncertainties and concerns. Many women have been able to acknowledge the fruitfulness of the waiting period and the long years of diaconate as lay workers, deaconesses or nuns. This acknowledgement is underlined in a special way by Jackie (Chapter 8), writing from the perspective of a Roman Catholic laywoman and called to the priesthood herself, she observes our Anglican processes while she meditates on her own. Her valuing of the waiting time makes poignant reading, since within her own Church there is little light to be seen yet at the end of that long tunnel. Likewise, the vote taken by the Church in Wales is another sadness to be borne.

For many women, this waiting period, whilst filled with frustration and difficulty, has also provided the space for the gifts of priesthood to be received. The act of priesting for them will have been only a validation of a priesthood already fulfilled in all but name. But for others the Church's decision to priest us was the moment when the real questions could be admitted and asked for the first time.

> Not knowing even that we're on the way
> Until suddenly we're there. How shall we know?

How *shall* we know we have asked ourselves? How *should* we find our way through the maelstrom of feelings released by the Church's own ambivalent invitation, to some more certain place beyond our own ambivalence? Now that the possibility was actually there before us, *did we really want it?* More crucially perhaps, *could we really bear it,* this terrible, painful, extraordinary gift, given to the Church and for the Church, but mediated through the fragility of our own individual spirits? And dared we allow ourselves now to ask such terrible disturbing questions? Are they not, we asked ourselves, an insult to all those who had for centuries participated in this struggle in their many different ways?

These are no doubt questions that have struck every potential male priest as he has tried to come to terms with the gulf between what is being offered and asked of him, and his own knowledge of who he really is. ('Lord, if it be thy will, may this

cup pass from me.' Who could desire to be drawn so closely into
the suffering humility of God through the priesthood of his
Son?) But in our particular case—the first group of women to
be priested in the Church of England—we must also bear the
weight of the expectations placed upon us by our supporters and
the equal burden of grief and disturbance that we witness in
those who oppose our vocation.

My own journey through the last two years has been particularly influenced by my membership of two very different groups.
The first was a group of women deacons who met at approxi-
mately three-weekly intervals during the period between the vote
and our ordinations in the Southwark diocese in May. This group
gradually became a safe place for some of these questions to be
raised and answered. But there were other questions that had to
be faced, by these and other women with whom I have talked.
The sudden psychic shift that took place in the organism as a
whole on 11 November seemed to release for some women suppressed experiences of abuse, encountered in both their personal
lives and in their long ministry as deacons in the Church. Now
that the Church was perceived as structurally less abusive to
their identity as women, they were able to begin to acknowledge
the awful backlog of pain that they carried from the complex
intertwining of various kinds of emotional and sometimes physical or sexual abuse. Experiences in the 'family' of the Church
had compounded for them the abusive experiences they had
encountered in their own original families. This raised, and continues to raise, the larger question: how can we who have been
damaged avoid in our turn becoming damaging to others? Will
entry into the priesthood compound the pain or simply change
us from victims to perpetrators in our turn? If so, how will this
be experienced? And how can it be avoided?

Abuse of any kind is experienced differently by women and
men because of the differences in their own developmental histor-
ies. The experience is also significantly different when the abuser
is herself a woman. Men are confronted again by their angry,
controlling and maybe abusive mothers from the past from whom
they nevertheless know themselves as 'different'. Women are also
confronted with their angry and maybe abusive mothers from
the past but, as well as the fear, there is also the disappointment

that she (the person 'like me' in gender terms) is nevertheless
an abuser. Both women and men look to mother to protect and
nurture, to absorb the panic and the fear. It is the reason why it
is so hard to accept the reality that mothers as well as fathers
can abuse their children, physically, sexually and emotionally. But
such knowledge is even I believe more difficult for a woman to
accept, because it carries with it the terrible disappointment that
nothing has changed and that the person 'like me' has been able
to do no better.

In her sharply critical contribution in Chapter 7, Maggie
explores what some of these questions might mean in relation to
women priests and her conclusions are pessimistic, perhaps
unfair. But they are one American laywoman's experience of
priestly women who have been unable sufficiently to manage
the meaning of their own abusive past when it meets with the
expectations that have been placed upon them as priests. They
have consequently become abusive to others in their turn. Identification with the aggressor is a very well understood psychological
defence. This unconscious imitation of the abuser by those whose
weak position has been suddenly changed may be rooted in
childhood or in the more recent experiences of having been
disempowered by the structures and individuals of a patriarchal
Church. Being more aware of these possibilities should lead us to
ask how we will ourselves avoid becoming narcissistic, excluding,
proprietorial and domineering in the expression of our priesthood
which, when exercised by others in this way, may have caused
such damage to us. The model of priesthood explored by
Maggie—the kenotic model of Christ—provides us with an image
of the utmost importance if we are to make our own woundedness
usable for others rather than take revenge on others for our own
wounds and scars.

It is a theme that Jane Williams takes up in a different way in
Chapter 6. One of the big changes during the past two years has
been the loosening of old solidarities and the creation of new
ones. There are things here to be grieved for as well as the
frisson of new possibilities. As Jane points out, women, lay and
ordained, who have worked alongside each other without distinction in the effort to open the priesthood to women, are now
divided by ordination itself. The first ordinations this year mean

a parting of the ways between women. How will this affect their relationships? Are ordained women going to provide a means whereby lay women become further empowered and released from their shackles, or will ordained women create new and more troubling oppressions for their sisters?

Lay women have been at the very heart of the movement for women's ordination. Will they now, like Jane's opening story about herself, feel excluded and betrayed? Will their own priestly identity and vocation in the Church be further eroded by this change? So much has been vested in the profound significance of this great symbolic step—'a small step for woman, but a giant leap for womankind'—all this has been confidently preached for decades. But the question remains: will women yet 'be disappointed in their hope' for all that they have believed in for themselves and for their sisters? 'If our sisters are involved in the processes that not only represent God to the world, but also misrepresent him, then we can no longer blame "the men", and assure ourselves that we could do it better' (p. 88). Or, will the hope be realized that ordained women can release lay women and lay women release ordained women in a mutual effort to find their voices and speak the words that they have been given to speak? Clare, in her chapter 'A resounding silence', describes the long road towards finding her own voice which had for so long been unexpressed. Her personal journey is the journey of so many women, as Gilligan (1982) and other feminist psychologists have described. The first ordinations mark in a powerful sense the 'finding of our voices'. But these few voices found will only have meaning as they become the opportunity for all women to sing their song of liberation.

There are also anxieties to be faced in this area amongst ordained women themselves. Up until now women in ministry have formed a small minority group (about 10 per cent at present) within the larger body of male clergy. An interesting question suggests itself as to whether women in ordained ministry have, consciously or unconsciously, been attracted to a Church where they are ministerially in the minority? This minority position has all sorts of compensations, especially when, in the body of the Church, the vast majority of the laity are women. May it not be much more confirming of one's sense of identity to become part of a small minority of the ordained, rather than sink without trace amidst the majority of the lay? If so, what will happen when, as Christine anticipates, 'the proportion of women to men in ordained ministry increases to the point where a better balance is achieved, and women are less of a minority' (p. 81)? Will the same kind of competitive envy that so bedevils male clergy emerge then with equal disruptiveness amongst women? Will some of the notions of consensus and collaboration, so powerfully experienced amongst women before the vote, turn out to be unsustainable in the scramble for jobs (for power and preferment and the other seven devils?) and in the desire to redress the injustices that have for so long kept ordained women servile? Will the burden of projections loaded upon *all* clergy as representative bearers of the pathology of others prove overwhelming, and ultimately prevent the high hopes and ideals for these womanly times from being realized? And will the despair that this engenders be too great to bear either by ourselves or by our unordained sisters? Jane Sinclair (Chapter 9) acknowledges the possibility that the advent of women may make the Church no less clericalized than it is already. But she also sees ways in which the liturgical role of the priest will hopefully point the way towards finding new meaning and new creativity when it is exercised by women.

My membership of a second group was equally important in enriching my recent experiences. This group met monthly from April 1992 and committed itself to continue until May 1994 when women were ordained in the Southwark diocese for the first time. The group was made up of four priests opposed to women's ordination and five women deacons who felt called to the priesthood. All four men were active in organizations that had taken a major part in spearheading the opposition to women's ordination and similarly, the women were either active in the Movement for the Ordination of Women or in other women's groups. The task of the group was simply to meet, to share experiences, to listen to the opposing view and, above all, to continue to meet together regularly before and after the vote, come what may. Members of the group committed themselves to pray for each other, to learn from each other and to create

and maintain a bond of charity between us which would super-
sede our passionately held differences.

The agenda explicitly excluded any effort to change each
other's views or even enlighten each other in any explicit way
regarding misunderstandings or misperceptions of the other's
position. For the first half of its life, the group was tightly
structured, to avoid it becoming a discussion group or entering
the arena of polemics or persuasion. Silence, prayer and creative
listening were important ingredients. Members sometimes felt
weighted down by the impasse of what was felt to be a useless
exercise—living out the experience of being together and bearing
the pain and anger of each person's own rejection, seen mirrored
in the face of those who seemed to be its cause. There was
perhaps a dawning realization at times that this was how things
were going to remain—a nailing to the cross—an experience of
prolonged immovability, with no light at all at the end of the
tunnel.

Undoubtedly, however, as the group developed a trusting life
of its own, and the quality and depth of sharing between its
members increased, each person also found that he or she was
growing and changing in relation to the others. In some ways
the experience doubled the pain and the complexity of the situation, because each member found it more difficult to project
and displace emotions onto the other or to distort the other's
beliefs or motivation. There was, too, a growing realization at
some level that the movements for and against the ordination of
women were opposite sides of the same coin, carrying meaning
for the whole Church and catalysing a new emotional working-
through of issues of gender, sexuality, power and personhood at
both individual and institutional levels.

Other parts of this chapter reflect something of the experiences
of the women in this group, too, as I have both perceived and
experienced them: the palpable movement discernible in some
women from positions of victims to 'victors' (and the complexi-
ties of that experience); the growing sense of empowerment and
rootedness in their own achievements and self-worth and an
increased understanding of how to hear the anger and pain of
others without taking personal responsibility for its cause. One
member described this as a shift to a place where she was able

to say 'I hear you, I have some understanding, but I do not accept personal responsibility for the stance you are taking'.

As the women deacons prepared for their ordination, the four men moved gradually towards their own resolutions of what was for them an appallingly painful crisis. One of the four came to feel that, partly because of his close experience of women deacons in the group, he had become able to reflect upon the church's situation in a new way and to feel that God was now opening new possibilities for his own ministry alongside women priests. A second felt that he should stay in the Church of England and continue to act as a focus for those who opposed the decision. From a new senior appointment in the diocese, he would play an important part in pastoring those who continued within the Anglican Church as well as trying to build bridges across the divide.

The third priest remained troubled and uncertain as to what he should do. He described his position as one of feeling immobilized, sometimes feeling he should leave, sometimes feeling he should stay. Two members of the group, a woman and a man, both faced the additional painful situation of finding themselves taking different positions from their marriage partners. These two members of the group were able to share with one another something of their own painful journeys and to give and gain considerable mutual support. He, the fourth priest member of the group, decided he should leave the Church of England and asked to be received as a Roman Catholic. As a married man, he and his wife faced losing their home, he the risk of losing his priesthood, and (as he and his wife held different theological positions on this issue) losing the unity of their spiritual experience. He wrote to his parish announcing his decision:

> I have had to take what may well turn out to be the most painful and difficult decision of my life . . .
> . . . those women who will be ordained . . . have a right, now that a decision has been taken, to expect their ministry to be accepted . . . I have respect for those who feel passionately that this is right; it is partly because of that respect that I feel the time is right for a loving and caring parting of friends.

*

Earlier we noted the dilemmas and difficulties for some women both in exercising the institutional priesthood and in receiving the ministry of women priests. There are great dilemmas for some men too. For some male priests, membership of an all-male priesthood has enabled them to function creatively and maturely in a secure environment. It has allowed them to exercise their compassionate, intuitive gifts amongst their largely female flocks alongside maintaining their male identity within their colleague group.

The significant differences in personality profiles noted by Francis (1991) in his comparison between both male and female ordinands, and the population as a whole, suggests that there is some reversal in terms of normative characteristics along the gender division, even when a necessarily cautious approach to the allocation of gender characteristics is taken. This suggests that some male clergy are experiencing a profound sense of invasion and attack at the prospect of so radical an alteration in the symbolism of priesthood. For them, the presence of priestly women may dilute the powerful reparative need which may lie deeply within their motivation in becoming priests. Their vocation has enabled them to 'make reparation' on behalf of their gender for the ills that are perpetrated by men upon women. This reparative possibility also allows men to sublimate their own violence and channel it instead through the 'violence' of the Eucharist. At the same time, the priesthood enables men to carry the 'feminine' pastoral functions of priesthood and to express those within a situation where most of the recipients are women and children. Thus the unintegrated parts of the male psyche are provided with rich opportunities for healing and growth.

The proximity of real women in the priesthood also robs men of their assumption of womanliness; it calls the bluff of this incorporation of the feminine. At the same time, it faces men too starkly and too closely with the reality of femininity which may be both longed for and feared. An all-male priesthood has allowed some men to shelter from the ambiguities of gender within a defensive structure which has provided a retreat from and a connection with the feminine simultaneously (Walrond-Skinner, 1992). Part of the shock of the Church's crisis is being borne most painfully by these men.

As I have watched men, in a variety of settings, trying to come to terms with things that cannot be explained but only felt, I have grieved with them for all that seems lost. I have witnessed the terrible longing of those who cannot accept what has happened and yet cannot bear the loneliness and pain and exclusion of their own position. I have watched as they have wept. And my arrogance has been humbled and I have been healed somewhat of my own scars. In the process I have prayed that the Body of Christ, in all its different parts, may gradually recover from its profound trauma, and break through into a new place of inspiration, freedom and grace.

This will not happen by argument; it will not happen by conscious efforts to change. It will not happen through reorganization, or through the redistribution of offices or opportunities within the structure of the Church. It will not come about through training or spirituality courses or books or conferences or decades dedicated to this or that aspect of the ministry of the Church. It will not come through missions and it will not come through campaigns. Nor will it come about even through the process of living the mystery of our own vocations—*unless*, at the heart of that vocation, lies the radical still centre of a life of prayer, fostered now with new and urgent vigour. Una, who holds a special place in the movement that has successfully resulted in the ordination of women in England this year, has important comments to make here (Chapter 10). She and Maggie both contribute to this book from the position of religious, living a contemplative life. Both, from their different perspectives, have become 'one of the spaces where Christ does his healing work of reconciliation' (p. 162). Both in their different ways invite us to do the same. Such may indeed prove to be the only way in which our new womanly times within the Church will become a real sign of hope for the transformation of the world.

> Not knowing even that we're on the way,
> Until suddenly we're there. How shall we know? . . .
>   All fears of present and future
> Will be over, all guilts forgiven
> Maybe, heaven. Or maybe
> We can get so far in this world. I'll believe we can.
>   (Fanthorpe, 1990)

References

U. A. Fanthorpe, 'Idyll' from *Neck-Verse* (Calstock, Cornwall: Peterloo Poets, 1992). These lines come from a whimsical little poem that caught my eye during various journeys on the London Underground.

L. J. Francis, 'The personality characteristics of Anglican ordinands: feminine men and masculine women?', *Personality and Individual Differences*, vol. 12 (1991), pp. 1133–40.

C. Gilligan, *In a Different Voice: Psychological Theory and Women's Development* (Cambridge, MA: Harvard University Press, 1982).

S. Walrond-Skinner, 'Reflections on the psychology of a male priesthood' in *Beyond Contradiction: Essays in Memory of Paul Baker, 1954–1989* (Bristol: Paul Baker Estate, 1992).

2

The guardian of the Grail

MONICA FURLONG

There is a law in life (which is something to do with the nature of fantasy) that by the time you get what you want—the prize job, the coveted place in an institution, the award—the great days of the profession or institution are already over, and everyone is into the head-shaking things-are-not-what-they-were stage. You have come too late. A friend of mine says that by the time he gets to heaven he is sure God will have left on a long vacation, and the whole place will be going downhill.

There is a hint of all this around women being priested in the Church of England. They have 'arrived' at a time when there is a dismal lack of leadership and vision, when there are acute financial problems and a shrinking number of jobs. A cold coming they have had of it, too: the Act of Synod was about the frostiest welcome imaginable.

But there is a further irony, or bitter twist, which is that the very arrival of women priests appears to separate the Church of England still further from its golden age or supposed ideal state. This is not just because it has thrown the whole organization into a game of Uproar. It is more to do with the effect women have, just by being there. I remember a shrewd priest suggesting to me in the very early days of the Movement for the Ordination of Women that as women entered any profession its status dropped, and that the priesthood would be no exception. As women eventually enter all the professions at the highest level this must, of course, cease to be so, and women's own status will gradually improve as they become associated with jobs that are highly respected, but in the interim they seem to reduce the admiration quotient of the job concerned. Like Groucho Marx, who wasn't sure he wanted to join the sort of golf club that admitted people like himself, i.e. Jews, some women priests may wonder if the priesthood they are entering is the sort of priesthood they dreamed about now that its mystique is diluted by many like themselves.

It is a bold claim for me to say that I see the above as cause for hope and rejoicing, but I do. In fact I could not feel more optimistic both for women and for the Church of England, though we are by no means out of the wood yet. This is because I sense that the Church of England is being pushed by the advent of women priests, much against its will, to reassess everything about its hierarchical and status-ridden and sexist attitudes. And in this distress it must turn back, as all believers must, to Christian origins and insights.

An analogy that I keep catching myself making in this context is that of the nervous breakdown. Suppose, I think to myself, that the Church, over the last fifteen years or so, has been having a nervous collapse. Now possibly it is in the final stages of the illness, or perhaps is making its first diffident steps back to normal life. In nervous breakdowns, as I understand it, people find themselves so at odds with themselves that they are unable to function. The sensible, 'coping' self, the 'ego' in psychological jargon, wants to get on with life ('There are far more important issues . . .'), go to work, continue relationships, present a smooth and competent front to the world. But another part of the self resists this, refuses to cope or to conform, and is unable any longer to keep up appearances. The will has temporarily collapsed, and the loss of control, with its accompanying sense of shame and humiliation, is evident to all. But there is also a powerful need to admit to sadness, disinterest, depression, fear, anxiety, dark fantasies, loss of hope and direction, and other worrying symptoms. The individual finds him- or herself in the extraordinarily painful position of being in a state of psychological civil war.

To the sick person this seems about the most terrible thing that could possibly happen, but the psychotherapist may see something very different. She may see someone who tried to

lead their life much too narrowly and timidly, suppressing and
ignoring huge desires and energies, probably as a result of early
trauma or harsh conditioning. Now those energies refuse to be
suppressed any longer, and in an internal earthquake, that cannot
be other than excruciatingly painful, the desires move into consciousness. 'This thing of darkness', as Prospero said of Caliban,
'I acknowledge mine.' Once the desire is admitted and accepted,
however unwillingly, and is seen not to be the sinister agent of
darkness, but simply a part of the self that needs a chance to
grow, a great change takes place. The person gradually begins
to live with an energy unknown before, and without the haunting
fears of 'the repressed' breaking through. Not immediately, but
slowly, life becomes much more joyful and zestful, and there is
a clearer sense of direction than for many years previously.

So if, as I believe, the Church of England has just passed
through something like this painful journey of self-discovery, and
is now trying to get its life together again, we may look for new
energy and ideas to emerge from the present poverty and rigidity.
I think there were observers at many stages—particularly on the
'opposition' side—who felt in their unhappy bones the way things
were going and who tried to stave off the inevitable. I remember
Archbishop Runcie, as long ago as 1980, telling us that if we
insisted on women's ordination it would 'split the Church'. He
was, I think, rebuking us for our 'selfishness' in insisting on
women's vocations, but I believe he saw, and feared, the suppressed energy implicit in them. He was prophetic because,
throughout the 1980s, the split continued to grow, and the voice
of protest grew shriller and more desperate.

Innumerable weak, almost comic, arguments were put forward
to block or postpone the inevitable—everything from women's
supposed physical and psychological frailty (a difficult thesis to
maintain while the Iron Lady was 'the best man in the Cabinet'),
to Graham Leonard's assurances that God was male.

As the defences began to be breached, protest came from every
direction: from Anglo-Catholics—'Women cannot be priests'; lib-
erals—'Of course I believe in women's ordination but the time
is not ripe'; Evangelicals—'The man is head of the woman';
senior Roman Catholics (possibly manipulated by Anglican
friends)—'This will set back the cause of ARCIC by years/

decades/centuries/in perpetuity'; by women themselves—'I don't fancy confessing to a woman'. It was handicapped too by women who were in favour of women's ordination, but who were so nervous of being seen as pushy, ungracious, aggressive or unfeminine, of upsetting the men, annoying the bishops, being scowled at in Synod, etc., etc., that it was difficult for them even to know what it was they really wanted, let alone to maintain it in the face of a barrage of ridicule and temper tantrums. Yet in spite of the heavy odds against it the ordination of women occurred.

There is a point where the inner pressure to change becomes so urgent that, whatever the cost, it becomes easier to go forward than to go back. I believe that the Church reached that point somewhere about 1986/87. First the measure which would have allowed women ordained abroad to celebrate in this country went down, then, in the next year, some leading churchmen, including Dr Runcie, who had been thought to favour women's ordination, suddenly voted against a measure designed to promote it. Many who previously had been rather complacently in favour of women priests, and comfortably sure the legislation would happen without any great commitment on their part, began to see that real effort would be needed if we were to overcome a by now well-orchestrated opposition.

From 1987, women deacons, quietly and effectively getting on with their jobs, also began to undermine the unthinking prejudice that had poisoned previous church attitudes. Resolve about the priesting of women hardened as it was recognized that change had to happen, and that it might be less damaging sooner than later. So in 1992 the legislation at last acknowledged that the inner revolution had really happened.

What had the Church's nervous breakdown all been about? What was 'the repressed' that is still returning painfully to consciousness, and which all the churches in time will have to deal with? What was 'the thing of darkness' that the Church had to recognize or sink into a half life? The need to distinguish themselves from the lascivious 'mystery religions' on the one hand, and the terrible impact of persecution on the other, drove the first Christians away from exploring the new attitudes towards women clearly implicit in the teachings of Jesus, which seem to have been tentatively tried out in the first Christian communities. Under stress people tend to return to the status quo, and the status quo was Jewish property and purity laws, or Greek and Roman ideas about female inferiority, which, according to some writers, e.g. William Countryman, have continued to dictate Christian attitudes to women until the present day. Within Jewish culture at least, with its powerful sense of heterosexual eroticism, gender attitudes may have had quite a different feeling. Within Christianity the legacy brought about a contempt for sexuality and the body, and an exaggerated emphasis on celibacy. Since to despise the body is to despise women's unique ability—that of giving birth—and to despise sexuality is to despise the one who inspires sexual desire, women were handicapped and downgraded in the new dispensation in a way that seems to have nothing to do with anything ever said or done by Jesus. Tragically, almost from the beginning, Christian relations between women and men were spoiled in the most fundamental way imaginable, by a belief in the inequality of the partners, so that erotic desire was subtly corrupted at the root by issues of power. The joy of 'making love' was infected by sado-masochistic fantasy, as is only too evident in Western eroticism to this day.

An interesting and relatively early recognition of a fatal distortion about sexuality within Christianity is the story of the Grail King, part of the huge body of Arthurian legend. Arthurian stories had began to collect during the Dark Ages, and to be written down for the first time in the early Middle Ages. The Grail story is told by Chrétien de Troyes in *Conte del Graal*, written in 1190. The stories are a complex, and often obscure, gloss and meditation on Christian myth, and in particular the myth of the quest for the Grail. They have the naïvety of fairy stories, but also the wisdom.

According to Chrétien de Troyes, the Grail King, or keeper of the Grail (which I take to be the Church), was maimed, or, in the euphemism of the medieval writers, 'wounded in his thighs', i.e. he was impotent. In primitive belief, the king's impotence means that his whole kingdom is sterile and devastated, a Waste Land. For healing to take place, and for the Waste Land to be freed from its sinister enchantment, a knight must survive extraordinary dangers to reach the palace of the Grail, and he must ask the king a crucial question. (In Malory's version of the Grail story, written three centuries later, the Maimed King is eventually cured by blood being smeared upon him.)

Who is the knight and what is the fateful question? In the manner of fairy tales the one who holds the key, the wisdom, is nearly always the one who is overlooked—the youngest child, or the one regarded as a negligible fool. Fairy tales repeatedly teach that in order to find the solution to our problems we should search at home rather than abroad (unknown to us, the treasure lies beneath the hearth stone), and that we should look to the neglected, the despised, the easy to ignore, the old woman gathering sticks on the edge of the forest, the beggar, the cripple, the mouse. Or, as the gospel puts it in what was probably a favourite Jewish proverb, 'The stone that the builders rejected is become the head of the corner'. Well, we do not have far to seek in Christian history to find the scorned and disliked 'other'.

Not long after the Arthurian legends began to cluster into written stories, the persecution of witches, which may well have been going on for centuries, began to be more organized, as the Church itself became more organized. Although there were a few male 'magicians', the persecution of witches was a pogrom almost entirely aimed at women. The last and most terrible of these holocausts took place in a seventeenth-century Europe torn apart by the Reformation. In France and Germany thousands of women were brutally tortured until they confessed and implicated thousands more. In England there were stricter rules about torture, but women, very often elderly, indigent, women who had no friends to complain on their behalf, were still subjected to swimming 'ordeals', 'pricked', i.e. searched for 'witches' teats' (warts) all over their bodies, which were then pierced, refused food and drink until they 'confessed', or 'walked' until they dropped from exhaustion. Convicted, they were burned to death, on the Continent and in Scotland, or hanged, in England.

The savagery with which these persecutions were pursued, for reasons which now seem to us almost entirely fictitious, suggest that 'the repressed', i.e. the power of sexuality and the body, the force of 'the feminine', and the power of women, was trying to return, to emerge from its relegation to obscurity and contempt, and that the persecutors were determined to deny it. Significantly

James I wrote a famous treatise about witches called *Demonologie* (1597) in which his principal accusation against them is that they caused impotence in men, 'weakening the nature of sane men, to make them unable for women'. James, we know, was homosexual, and in his struggles to produce heirs he must have cast around for someone to blame for his difficulties. Women were the scapegoats, as they were also scapegoats for plague, sudden death and the failure of crops. (It is said that to this day, in French kitchens, menstruating women are blamed if the sauce curdles.) What is suppressed and denied, in this case the full recognition of women as people, becomes a threat. It is not a far cry from this to the speakers in General Synod in 1984 who spoke of women 'destroying' and 'disembowelling' the Church, or as 'a virus in the bloodstream'. The voice of the Witchfinder General still echoes in our ears.

So it is that when women, menstruating, gestating, or otherwise, stand at last at the Christian altar and hold the body and blood of Jesus in their hands, they may become the key which will resolve the suffering of the Church, bring greenness to its life, naturalness to its manner, health to its thinking, energy to its theology and laughter to its lips. I am not, of course, speaking here of the special qualities of any of the new women priests, remarkable as some of them are, but rather of the subtle change that will occur simply by reason of their 'being there' and being women. They may reduce the supposed 'status' of priesthood (no bad thing), while bringing a far greater gift that as yet we can scarcely guess at. But 'sexuality' and 'spirituality' will be seen to be present together at the altar, rather like righteousness and mercy embracing one another. *There* is healing, whether we consciously recognize it or not. The unknown knight, female in this case, after so many adventures, finds the Grail Castle, approaches the Grail King, and puts the vital question, which is something like 'Do you want to recognize the part of yourself which you believe to be dark, fearful, inferior, secret, feminine? Do you want to acknowledge this thing of darkness? It has caused so much pain, so much shame, but it too is of God. Embrace me, and you will be well.' And so women, all women, not just women priests, of course, become the new guardians of the Grail.

Because of the importance of the woman priest as symbol it

was crucial that the ordinations actually happened; it would not
have been enough, as Synod speakers were fond of suggesting,
simply for women's ministry to be 'recognized' in some slightly
patronizing way that fell short of priesthood. Yet it is vital that
the woman priest does not become a victim of the 'inflation', or
over-valuation of herself, which priests sometimes seem to reveal.
A model that strives for the naturalness and quiet integrity of
Chaucer's 'poor parson', himself trying to emulate the simplicity
of Christ, seems a more appropriate pattern for all priests.

If male priests have sometimes been guilty of an inflated idea
of themselves and their powers, it is not entirely their fault.
Frequently it has seemed to be women, striving at secondhand
for a power and influence that has been denied to them, who
have flattered the ego and over-valued the mystique of male
priests, and thus helped to bring the inflation about. There is
much work to be done in re-visioning and articulating the role
of the priest, and I long for the day when women have enough
experience of it to be able to tell us what it is like and how they
see themselves.

Part of the paradoxical importance of the priest at this point
is that the laity are only now emerging into their full importance.
The arrival of women priests coincides with a process of lay self-
discovery. They are no longer the 'simple faithful' (well, they
would do well not to be) but an educated group who may know
as much, or more, theology than the priest. If women priests
know what is good for them they will control any dog-in-the-
manger tendencies they may have, any longings to be part of a
mandarin caste, and they will encourage the rise of the laity.
This is partly because 'enabling' is the only evangelical path now
open, but there is also a more political reason which is that the
laity will keep liberty alive in the Church. In a Church where
the parson's freehold is sinking into disuse, and in which, for the
first time in my memory, clergy are becoming anxious about
losing jobs or job opportunities if they speak out bravely, it is
becoming very evident that the laity alone have the vital freedom
to criticize or dissent.

I must confess to a personal hope, born partly out of the
Church's acute financial crisis, which is that the priesting of
women may also usher in a kind of 'small is beautiful' church.

I am repelled by the increasingly monolithic feel (though much less oppressive in the Church of England than in the Roman Catholic Church), the sense of impersonal machination on the one hand, and of 'official pronouncements' on the other. If at all possible I would much rather see a sort of 'cottage industry' church, in which nearly all the reference is local, and in which the major purpose is to overcome the loneliness of modern life, and also to help a particular group to work out the morals of its own life experience. (I cannot forget the sermon of an Asian priest that I listened to in a Tower Hamlets church the weekend after Tower Hamlets elected a council member from an avowedly racist party. Here was something about as far from an official pronouncement as you could get—a man speaking out of his own pain and the pain of those he ministered to.) 'Official pronouncements', in contrast—about homosexuality, divorce, abortion, euthanasia, war, crime, or whatever it may be—always seem to be a long way from the front line where the real questions have to be faced and the solutions found. They are a pretence to power where there is no power, yet their ripples go out to cause pain to people who are forced to resolve impossible dilemmas in order to live their lives at all. Of course, the Church is always under pressure, particularly from the Conservative Party, to issue moral statements, particularly if they agree with Conservative doctrine. But there is no need to bow to such pressure. Anyway, I hope women will be less judgemental and have less need for the sort of illusory 'control' which so often seems to permeate church attitudes; they may be realistic enough to recognize that the Church no longer has that sort of influence except on a very few people, and those few, still stuck in the mould of 'good children', are not necessarily the most creative and adventurous in our society.

I hope too that women will be bold in theological discussion. We already have a number of very distinguished women theologians in key jobs in the universities. It would be good if they could manage to communicate their ideas in language that lay people might understand. I have felt rather disappointed in this so far, and cannot decide whether it is simply that academic language automatically deadens communication, so that people who once wrote well learn to become boring, or whether women academics are hell-bent on playing the male game better than the men. Either way, it is not going to get us anywhere. We need plain language, bold and creative thinking, and an awareness of an audience that stretches beyond the quadrangle and the campus.

As a feminist I long to see feminist ideas gain ground in the Church, since I am frequently shocked at the way even basic ideas about equality, already a commonplace in business and industry, seem to come as a shock to Synod and the bishops. The Church has everything to learn in establishing a simple and basic equality between men and women, and the longer it takes to do it the more foolish it appears.

Yet I feel that feminists must themselves be careful of a sort of barbarism which rejects all the achievements of Christianity in the eras before women were liberated. The achievements, however flawed by ignorance and sexism, were still marvellous, a great fountain of life and art which only fools would despise.

Nobody really knows whether women have a different 'spirituality' from men, and what difference this might make to the sort of Church they will help to build. The one thing that does seem certain is that women's 'experience' historically has been totally different from men's, away from the huge dramas of politics and war, and primarily concerned with bearing and cherishing life. We live in an age in which, if we cannot learn to cherish life, in all its forms, and give up war, then the species and the planet itself is doomed. It is surely no accident that this is the time when 'the feminine' (in men, of course, as well as in women) steps forward to guard the Grail.

Men, as well as women, need to take on the cherishing of life—to value both its beauty and its cost to the women who give birth. Nothing has been sadder in the films of Yugoslavia and other war-ravaged countries than the sight of elderly women who, in losing their beloved children in the war, have lost their whole life's endeavour.

If relations between men and women can be equal, with a love and eroticism that is not fired by dominance, then perhaps we are on our way to a richer sexuality, to a new way of bringing up children, of valuing life in a way that will help us to reject war, and of being more tolerant of people who are different from us—racially, sexually, religiously. Is this what women priests are all about? I certainly hope so.

3

A resounding silence

CLARE HERBERT

... every man heard them speak in his own language.
Acts 2.6

In our family album there is a photograph of me aged five,
wearing a blue and white striped dress, reciting a poem about a
dormouse who lived under a toadstool. Miss Pritchard, my first
teacher, elderly and portly, is holding me, her prize pupil, on a
little stage. My brother, my senior at school, sits watching,
crouched with other children on the floor. Mr Vicarage, a white-
haired school governor, stands impatiently to one side, holding
his master of ceremonies programme as if waiting to get on. My
mouth is hardly open, my face a picture of earnest concentration.

I am grateful for the existence of that photograph. I can
remember quite clearly the blue and white dress. It had pink
carnations along the white stripes and was a gift from my aunt
in Sheffield. I rarely saw that aunt but she sent large and promis-
ing parcels in brown paper at regular intervals, containing Callard
and Bowser sweets, dresses for me and jumpers for my brother.
And I have a slight memory of the poem itself. But I would not
remember the feelings evoked by the occasion if it were not for
the existence of that photograph.

For at quite another level the picture shows that for me a
mysterious event has occurred. No one had asked me beforehand
to recite and here I am grappling for the first time in public
with the question of who I am! Why was I speaking, and not my

brother? Why was my trustworthy teacher singling me out of my circle? Was there some mysterious link between enjoying reading poems and being asked to do this? There was enough time in the sand-tray days, between 'Janet and John' books and sum-cards about coconut shies, to learn poems by heart, so I knew the work. But faced with the need to declare my learning publicly I couldn't find the words.

Out of my mouth came only a thin whisper, the waif of a sound.

While knowing the material about which I wish to speak I have found speaking itself difficult.

Nor did it seem that all the problems were solved by deciding to practise. As an undergraduate I enjoyed performing in light opera, but found it hard to convince myself that such frivolous activity was as valuable as study. Study absorbed me, but I found the razor-sharp discussion in theological seminars created conflict for me because of appearing 'brighter' than certain boyfriends. Proceeding to study pastoral theology my practical training centred on being trained with men to listen, rather than being trained as a woman to speak! By the end of my postgraduate days, I had learned to listen and write, but was advised by my male tutor not to attempt a doctorate until my spoken thoughts matched my written ideas in their confidence and clarity. The public utterance of thoughts and ideas was considered important, but the inner confidence to speak remained lacking.

In an article 'Meeting at the crossroads: women's psychology and girls' development', Lyn Mikel Brown and Carol Gilligan explore the stories of Anna and Neeti and the difficulty in learning to speak experienced by many young women (Brown and Gilligan, 1993). Both Anna and Neeti were students at the Laurel School for girls in Cleveland, Ohio, during the years 1986–90 and took part in a five-year longitudinal study of the psychological development of young women involving 100 girls between the ages of 7 and 18. Anna is a scholarship student and grows through adolescence with the knowledge that there is a wide gap between her family life at home and the idealized pictures of middle-class family life represented by her class-mates, what Anna calls the 'Polyanna' or 'Peaches and Cream' view of reality.

At the age of 12 Anna is passionate about knowing. She is beginning to sense that expressing feeling is important but not always a step towards fitting in and being popular. 'Though', Anna says, 'sometimes I'm mad at the world', she concludes, 'it's better to stay out of things, because people can get mad if you say something' (Brown and Gilligan, 1993, p. 18).

At 13 Anna seems to have gone underground. She speaks of 'keeping things to herself, of bringing herself out 'just a little bit' of 'playing a part' and of 'fitting into her new school' (p. 19).

At 14 Anna has become outspoken and has begun to value her own experience as a useful tool for understanding the world. Able to realize that her own view is valuable, she is also able to recognize the authenticity of different opinions. Asked 'What is society's image of the ideal woman?' she asserts 'Everybody has a different idea. I think everybody would have their own, and so there wouldn't be one image' (p. 22).

Through the course of her adolescence Anna admits that she is confused, particularly by the superficiality of many people's lives and their ambivalence towards speaking the truth as they see it. She resolves this confusion, in part at least, by finding a political voice with the support of a group of friends who are political resisters like her.

Neeti, at the age of 12, is also outspoken. She recalls to the interviewer an incident in which she has known her own feelings of concern, indignation, moral courage and self-confidence. Away at camp with a young cousin who is painfully homesick she defies the camp director's strict rules about phoning home and helps her cousin make contact with his parents. Like Anna at 12, she watches and listens, realizing there are patterns in people's behaviour which will provide signals about who they are and where she, Neeti, can 'fit in'. But Neeti's watching leads to wanting to respond to everything she sees, in a caring manner, in order that class-room relationships may go smoothly. Seeing that some people are alone, she tries 'to be friends' with most people. And Neeti feels good about her responsiveness to others: 'I feel good when there is a person and she doesn't have anybody to be with that day, so I stay with her and I feel good' (p. 25).

Unlike Anna, Neeti is starting to believe that it is best always to cover up negative feelings. It's really rude to be mean, she tells her interviewer, and so 'I just smile all the time'. Neeti wants to be recognized for who she is, at 12, and not for how popular she has become, but she is beginning to enjoy the power of being chosen, producing perfect class marks, active in sports, and behaving differently, she believes, around boys: 'I don't know if they'd like me for me, but I don't know if I act like myself, I can't tell.'

At the age of 13, Neeti shows that she has moved further out from being able to speak her own voice. She speaks in a passionless way about learning, despite attaining high grades: 'I just think that school is something, the only reason I am learning all this is to get into college and that's the only reason I am here' (p. 26).

Struggling to live up to images of female perfection, and never speaking to anyone in a remotely hurtful way, Neeti is already finding it difficult to find and express herself in a closer relationship with a class-mate. This class-mate is the daughter of her mother's friend, whom Neeti herself detests and whom she perceives as very unpopular in class. Neeti's paralysing dilemma is 'that I don't like this girl at all, that I absolutely hate her, but I don't know how to act because I have to be nice' (p. 27).

At 14 Neeti no longer speaks to her interviewer about bad feelings, anger or hatred. She continues, with little agony now, to be nice to the class-mate she dislikes, and carefully scrutinizes her friends and relationships for any sign of conflict. Neeti holds her real self apart from the expression of that self and becomes a mirror of what others want her to think. But her voice is weak. She has difficulty voicing anything but the nice and kind self she shows the world. Her response to how she has changed since the age of 12 is thin, as she realizes 'how important school is and how important friends are' (p. 28).

I have commonly experienced my own inner world as that of Neeti, feeling so silenced by the need to be nice that my feelings have been lost. But to become an Anna is to risk another sort of silencing. For fine voice though she has, Anna knows that she will probably only be able to exist comfortably well outside the mainstream political life of America: 'I'll live at the bottom of a mountain in Montana, just one of those weird people' (p. 29).

*

Very few deacons have spoken out publicly about their vision of themselves as priests, and I see in that silence a reflection of the need to be nice, to avoid stirring up turbulent feelings in the self or in the community of the Church, as if such feelings cannot be tolerated. There *is* another voice, that of Anna. But how is Anna to come back from Montana? Having found our Anna's voice in Womanchurch, in secular feminism, and in tasks and groups around the margins of the Church, how shall we speak with integrity at the centre? Is it possible to do so?

This chapter is an exploration of why we have been so silent. In tracing the history of the discovery of my own voice, and my own vision of priesthood, I link the silence in women with the developmental phase of adolescence. Leaving adolescence behind, whether in our individual selves or as a group of women in the Church, will require coming to terms with our anger, using the rebellious creativity we have discovered on the margins and discovering a confident silence which allows the voiceless to speak.

It was once I had left university, when I entered a secular job for the first time, that I was to discover my own voice. I was reading the writings of Thomas Merton and found myself exploring the theme of the mercy of God. Floundering around with no intimate relationships to bind me, nor any clear direction to my career, I came across these words:

> Mercy . . . is the bass bell and undersong of the whole Bible.
> Chesed (mercy) is also fidelity, it is also strength. It is ultimate
> and unfailing because it is the power that binds one person to
> another, in a covenant of hearts. It is the power that binds us
> to God because He has promised us mercy and will never fail
> in His promise. For He cannot fail. It is the power and the
> mercy which are most characteristic of Him, which come nearer
> to the mystery into which we enter when all concepts darken
> and evade us.
>
> (McDonnell, 1989)

I was about to discover mercy, outside the Church rather than inside it, to be grabbed by the urgent need to be merciful and in doing so to receive mercy. While recognizing the priestly task of displaying mercy to belong to the whole human community, I was to emerge from this next stage as one who understood her own priesthood to be about a willingness to be a singer of the undersong.

It was the freezing winter of a council workers' strike in Edinburgh. Rubbish sealed in mounds on the pavements made walking hazardous in the dark. I trudged daily to my job, past breweries, up towards Bruntsfield, down through Morningside to the corner of Morningside Drive. There at 6.30 I met a gang of women huddled in a shop doorway, waiting for a bus to take us up the long drive to the psychiatric hospital which stood like a faded baronial home on a hill on the edge of Edinburgh. Later, when the year turned and I was happier, I realized with a surge of wonder on what a magnificent site this hospital was built. On summer mornings I could see boats on the Firth of Forth, gleaming in the distance, and Arthur's Seat, the 'Lion Couchant', against pink and gold clouds. The view is breaktaking. But such mornings lay many months and several wards away. After two stints in psycho-geriatric wards I was now working as an auxiliary nurse in a long-stay ward for male patients, politely called an 'assessment ward': I saw no patient leave.

At 7.00 in the morning I would unlock the door of the ward to find George [a pseudonym] coming towards me. Some days he came roaring along, arms flailing, lost in painful memories of the war in Africa in which he had seen action. On calmer days we would dance along the shining corridor. I was unused to men, unused to dancing, but I danced. What else was there to do?

There was little room for inhibition. Days were filled with washing, food distribution, bathing, shaving and, occasionally, the calming of violence. I grew accustomed to thinking of a catatonic body in the toilet or the bath as a Christ-figure. Far harder for me to stomach was the expectation that on some occasions strong-arm tactics were necessary to make patients obey ward rules. I found myself gaining little respect from the staff in refusing to use them, but found a voice of resistance which felt my own. Similarly, I detested the boring routine of the days; men washed and dressed sitting around the walls seemed an appalling waste of time and life. I struggled to play games and to go out for walks, resisting the awful temptation to become glued to a chair in the duty room, which to me would mean refusing to accept the humanity of these men. It would have been so easy to do that, to deny that we shared the same human need of diversion, fun and adventure. I must have appeared eccentric at times as I struggled to find ways of communicating. The men had suffered alcoholism and psychotic illness, but in addition were institutionalized to the point of expecting no life outside the hospital ward.

I was fascinated by the work but was also afraid most of the time, afraid of outbursts of violence, afraid of feeling lonely among the staff, afraid that this clean and tidy scene was in fact the only possibility for these men's lives, that I was somehow 'silly'. Nevertheless, a voice of resistance was growing and making its presence felt.

Attending church, I remember clearly, gave me no way of breaking through my shyness or talking of all that was happening. I attended a famous church where I loved the liturgy and the good sermons of the priest-in-charge. How fluently he spoke, a spotlight posed in a theatrical way above his head in the dim building. All seemed order, form and beauty there, and I found no way to link the two worlds. 'Kingdom' and 'Church' were having little to do with each other for a while, as I glimpsed that a 'successful' institution was the last place I would find room for my confusion, pain and vision. My salvation was coming from elsewhere.

Everything that there was no opportunity to say in Church, there was space to say to a new and temporary staff member, a probation officer on placement in the hospital. She and I quickly formed a firm understanding of each other and of possibilities for more interesting work on the ward. In the transformation of my work life with her coming, and in the small changes we effected, together with other staff, in the lives of the men who were patients, I glimpsed the need for expressed vulnerability, and the acceptance of mutual dependence, in the experience of salvation.

With small groups of patients we began to take long walks. We ate out in a cafe in Morningside. As a ritual of rebellion we would throw stale hospital food to the ducks in Brayford pond and afterwards go for a beer. One ward sister took a group to a holiday camp, deciding that the new clothes and the excitement of the sun were worth it in themselves, even if memory-loss prevented the trip having lasting effect for some patients. I felt there could be no greater practice of the idea of 'the sacrament of the present moment' than that, to insist on good quality in the minutes of lives where hours were soon forgotten.

One evening my colleague and I were sitting around chatting and sewing in the living room. Some men were bantering with each other, and one patient whose only words took the form of the reiteration of a few short stories about his life was repeating these to a new friend who could tolerate the repetition. I glanced around and knew with one of those 'penny dropping' realizations, which seemed somehow to engage the whole body, that this way of being, this struggling to create a merciful community, had something to do with the peace and beauty of God. I knew in that moment that disorder, disease, lack of beauty and ability do not necessarily mar the image of God in us. Rather, it is often what we do to each other in our lack of acceptance and appreciation of each other which mars the 'heaven-being' of this world and puts us into hell.

When I was leaving the hospital I was asked to conduct a communion service, using the reserved sacrament, for the patients. That Eucharist, which patients interrupted with signs of boredom, affection and sheer bloody-mindedness, and which staff members who had shared grinding work with me attended, seemed a celebration of our common and vulnerable humanity, existing in, and struggling towards, the everlasting loving-kindness, the 'Chesed' of God.

It is no coincidence that my voice flourished afterwards, particularly in the creation of sermons, lectures and lasting friendships, when I entered theological college. In finding my place in a disordered world, I had begun the task which underlies the ability to be merciful and to receive mercy. I had begun to make connections with disordered parts of my own self, and so found that I could speak out in seemingly less disordered places. I still find myself stumbling over words and creating fantastic sentences, especially if excited or unprepared to speak. But the long adolescence of little connection between my inner world and my outer world was over.

It is my joy that with ordination to the priesthood women will be able to speak more clearly of their hopes and visions, released from a 'long adolescence' in the structures and decision-making processes of the Church. For, so far, we have been largely silenced. It is striking how, in the period between the vote in November 1992 and our ordination as priests in 1994, the institution of the Church has created very little space, if any, for the public proclamation of women's dreams and visions. We have done some work on our own, of course, and quietly. But while other women—theologians, journalists, and prominent lay people—have spoken and written of their protest and their hope, as deacons we have felt able to say very little.

My sense of the group of women deacons is that our prolonged adolescent period has tended to silence our dreams, because we are frightened of the anger we have been caused to feel in the past and in the present, and are scared to voice its depth. We have sought resolution for our conflict by 'privatizing our dreams', being priests in secret, in home groups, friendship groups, feminist circles, and while strengthened by this action we have not dared to speak much about it in the public places of the Church. This formation of identity, gained through studying theology and making liturgy with other women, has led to a third reason for silence about our future dreams. Discovering solidarity with secular feminists, and realizing the depth of sexism existing still, in all our institutions, we wonder if we dare dream! Will we be so absorbed into the hierarchical structures of a patriarchalist church that we lose our identity as a people of protest and become competitive, oppressive and less in touch with our need to receive mercy?

It is an urgent matter that we be freed from our silence to make theology, liturgy and structures for the renewal of the Church. Otherwise we may find ourselves running away, like Anna to Montana, unable to cope with the conflict involved in raising a political voice, or settling down, like Neeti, to a definition of ourselves designed by the need to 'fit in' with a male institution.

An essential step in being freed is examining and understanding our silence, so while the stories, visions and dreams of women are also found in this book I content myself with pausing to understand the difficulty of the task, for some of us, so that understanding it we may find ways to equip ourselves and support each other as our priestly ministry unfolds.

In 1983, while preparing to deliver a series of lectures on the development of feminist theology to students attending the extramural department of Bristol University, I puzzled over whether we would be able to stomach these words from Mary Daly:

> Virginia Woolf, who died of being both brilliant and female, wrote that women are condemned by society to function as mirrors, reflecting men at twice their actual size. When this basic principle is understood, we can understand something about the dynamics of the Looking Glass society . . . recognising the ineptitude of females in performing even the humble Feminine tasks (of feeding, washing and consoling) . . . the Looking Glass priests raised these functions to the supernatural level in which they alone had competence. In order to stress the obvious fact that all females are innately disqualified from joining the Sacred Men's club the Looking Glass priests made it a rule that their members should wear skirts.
>
> (Daly, 1986)

I myself was scared by the sarcasm of this long, hilarious outworking of Virginia Woolf's idea, and by the anger which lay behind the sarcasm. Yet women have good cause to be angry and, as the course developed, we were often deeply shocked by the treatment of women in history and by their representation in philosophical, religious and literary writings.

We saw how, before the Greeks established their dominance in the Aegean, Mediterranean thought was characterized by ideas of there existing a feminine divinity at the centre of the natural world, with nature ordered in natural cycles of growth and decay, sexual reproduction esteemed as a kind of immortality, and with the regular cycles of family life recognized as the basis of social and natural order. With the Greeks, women were effectively silenced, as Andrea Nye shows in her book *Words of Power*:

> Instead of a creative force at the centre of natural existence, a supreme warrior-father god Zeus legislated and punished from above and outside natural life. Order was a matter of law, and law reflected not the balance of reciprocity of natural process,

but the orderly dichotomies of hierarchicalized social structures
that had been divinely ordained. By law, man ruled woman
and Greek ruled barbarian and nothing should be allowed to
disturb the precarious order of those hierarchies.

(Nye, 1990, p. 17)

By the time of Plato, that 'nothing' included the free speech of
women:

> If a woman or servant insists on speaking to a man she, or he,
> can be required to follow proper logical form. She can be
> required to listen and to punctuate the speaker's remarks with
> signs of approval and acceptance. If she attempts to speak on
> her own, she can be accused of lack of rigour and lack of
> understanding of the categories of rational expression. If she
> ventures a thought outside the tree of logical concepts she can
> be dismissed and ridiculed as Theaetetus was by the Stranger.
> Better she can disappear altogether, leaving the world of public
> speech to men exercising their power over other men with
> their vision fixed on truth regardless of what she might say.

(Nye, 1990, p. 37)

Greek writers regularly referred to the inferiority of women;
to their babbling, emotionality and lack of courage. Because of
their natural inferiority, women's virtue was submission to the
superior rule of men in the family, not courage, let alone elo-
quence. It is no great step from this position to the world of
Neoplatonic thought to which St Paul spoke, in which women
were ordered to be silent in church and submit themselves to
the will of their husbands.

Not only were women being effectively silenced in all public
life, but equally any display by them of emotion was seen as a
sign of weakness. According to Aristotle's *Politics*, 'logic' was
understood as a way to identify 'that one who can plan things
with his mind' and is therefore 'the ruler by nature'. Women,
slaves, workers and conquered people, all those who did not
participate in dialectical contests, were expected to accept the
superior reasoning of their masters. Given this, Andrea Nye
writes how:

> An ethics can be theorized based on the authority of reason
> over emotion which is the mark of a man; a politics can be
> developed that founds men's authority over women and slaves

on the basis of that same rationality, other natural creatures
can be divided into lower species in imitation of the superior
species man; and finally divinity itself can be theorized as a
non material, manly intelligence removed from the distortions
of matter.

(Nye, 1990, p. 57)

This is not the place to recount the shockingly humiliating
pictures of women, their bodies and minds, their emotions and
ideas to be found in the early Church and in medieval theology.
Nor am I much comforted by the theology of the Reformation,
with its exhortations to women, being weak, that they should
play a restricted role in human affairs. By the time we had
completed the historical development section of my course in
feminist theology we were angry like Mary Daly, and found a
welcome release in laughter as we looked again at her images,
which now seemed mild.

The importance of understanding the historical development
of women's positions in Church and society for me has lain in
glimpsing why women may often feel so lacking in self-confidence
and self-assertion, almost as if we cannot accept that we are real
persons. Andrea Nye is speaking here of the thought world
of Philip and Alexander. But in the painstaking withdrawal of
women from public life, and the demeaning of her emotional
and intellectual life, so that she cannot own herself to be a
valuable citizen, I sense the evil of the dehumanization of women,
of which the modern Church is also guilty.

Once rationality is defined as what is not emotional, and
emotionality established as the characteristic of women, once
rationality is seen as a characteristic of mind, not body, and a
slave is understood as what is only a body, there could be no
discussion of the institutions of slavery or sexism.

(Nye, 1990, p. 50)

The proper reaction to such oppression is anger, which gives
us the energy to fight. I have always felt particularly angry when
the right of women to be ordained deacon or priest has been
voted on by a PCC, or by a predominantly male synod. I cannot
remain in the room, or listen to arguments which make of me
some object, whose fate can be decided upon by a group of

people perfectly happy to accept my priestly work, as long as it is not called that. I feel completely depersonalized by such debate about myself and have never understood friends who can bear to attend and follow the speeches avidly. I know that the anger of other deacons is sparked by different events, particularly by having to stand aside week by week as male priests celebrate the Eucharist, and by the persistent use of all-male language in the liturgy and hymnody of our Church.

It is not easy to feel free in expressing this anger, and often we have tried to hinder its expression in ourselves and in each other. Recently I attended a meeting of the London deacons while we were waiting to hear if we could be ordained priest at all in the London diocese. The air of the meeting was heavy and depressed, women finding it difficult to express their sense of powerlessness, until one by one they described the difficult and often ridiculous situations in which they were finding themselves. The parish priest in one woman's parish could not accept her ordination to the priesthood, while the PCC were supporting her. Other women were working effectively in parishes where the PCC felt unsure whether they should be ordained or not. One woman required certain medical insurance cover to work in the context of a particular institution, and couldn't receive it because she was not permitted to be called a chaplain! I felt exceedingly angry and was not surprised the meeting felt so leaden. These women were not being weighed up by 'strangers'; they were suffering rejections from the very people among whom they live and work every day. Yet it was hard for them to voice their anger. Complaining about this to friends and colleagues who were there, afterwards, one said that the silence was unusual, they were a group in waiting, while another said that we should be quiet, pray, and not rock the boat until we have all been ordained. But for whom were we being quiet that day, I wondered, since no male priest and few members of the Great Synod were present? Were we not, rather, afraid of expressing our real emotions, even to each other, and particularly the emotion of anger, that we should be waiting at all?

Alastair V. Campbell, in his book *The Gospel of Anger*, reveals how difficult it may be to express or even feel anger as a Christian: 'Christians feel uneasy with an angry God—and with their angry selves—and so, like children seeing ghosts in bedtime shadows, their fear of that which they only half understand and are too frightened to look at grows and grows' (Campbell, 1986).

He is quick to understand how people who concern themselves with pastoral work, who are drawn to devoting their whole lives to a Gospel of love may find it frighteningly difficult to admit the power of their own anger, thus blocking any consideration of an anger which may exist in God: 'Schooled as we are in the virtues of empathy, non-possessive warmth and unconditional acceptance we cannot easily serve the punishing God' (Campbell, 1986, p. 2).

I found myself remembering so many situations when I had been hurt by a sexist remark but dared not admit the hurt, distancing myself from the pain by hurriedly reinterpreting the situation and blaming myself for overreacting. Campbell describes reactions to a hurtful remark so well: 'Am I being too sensitive? Perhaps I should check it out with someone else. I certainly feel angry, but the insult may have been unintended. In my case, what should I do about it? I don't want a slanging match—or do I?' (Campbell, 1986, p. 26).

There is evidence that women, schooled in our society to please others in looks, dress and behaviour from an early age so that they successfully 'fit' with life in a male-dominated world as they mature, may have particular difficulty in expressing negative emotion. Neeti of the Gilligan and Brown study pleads that she cannot confront a friend with the truth as she sees it: 'because it would hurt her if I was honest. In such situations I think it's better to be nice since she might have been a little angry with me if I was honest with her' (Brown and Gilligan, 1993, p. 28).

As deacons we are used to being care-givers and may have been motivated to do the job initially, despite the difficult climate for women in the Church, because we come from families where we won our identity by care-giving and not by 'rocking the boat'. Anger with the Church may constitute an enormous threat of separation from that body of people which gives us so firm an identity, and so we tend to quell our doubts and crossness.

Moreover, still other influences work to diminish any confidence we have in our rightness in being angry. Women throughout the world are despairing of hope for a peaceful future. We have reason to be terrified of anger when we see the wars of aggression which rip the world apart, and the wholesale murder which takes place in the name of 'freedom', 'peace' and 'justice'. We feel caught in a trap, angry with the narrow visions of men concerning us and our world, yet fearing to fight back, join their game, become aggressive in our tone and being.

Part of my vision of priesthood is that as people of mercy we be merciful to ourselves and to each other. This will require us knowing our own anger when we are hurt, but being able to use aggression in a benign way, so that the other knows of the hurt, and relationship can be restored. Releasing our true selves in more honest, imaginative and co-operative ways will be a means to confronting the malignant aggression which threatens the destruction of peaceful society not only 'over the sea and far away' but on our own streets where people feel desperately purposeless, unrooted and unaffirmed as human beings. As women we need to learn that there is a difference between the anger which *heals* relationships, intimate and global, and the anger which enjoys the *destruction* of relationships, intimate and global. We must learn, in George Herbert's words, to 'lament *and* love' in the Church if we hope to become more truly merciful in the world.

> I will complain, yet praise;
> I will bewail, approve;
> And all my sour-sweet days
> I will lament, and love.
> (George Herbert)

Mary Grey well describes this middle path in her book *The Wisdom of Fools?*:

> Connected knowing does not flee difficult alternatives by flight into false innocence (I wash my hands of this mess) or forcible control (send in the troops). Connected knowing emerges from a way of experiencing the world in all its complexity and ambiguity.
>
> (Grey, 1993)

Sometimes as deacons we have been asked to 'not experience' the world, to separate ourselves off from our feelings of being frustrated, hurt and angry. We have learnt not only how to silence the expression of our feelings, but also how to 'not feel'. This has been one reason for finding silence-breaking hard.

A second reason for the silence of women deacons concerning our vision of our priesthood lies in our growing awareness of discovering another Church living alongside the institutional Church. If we have not agreed with the line of keeping quiet and not rocking the boat, with working patiently and steadily so that we convince people of our suitability for priesthood on account of our steady character, then we have formed and joined alternative Churches. Alongside the mainstream churches there has grown up Womanchurch.

For myself, participation in Womanchurch has brought the discovery of liturgy as a pastoral event. The awareness that language which includes the experience of women, stories which repeat the experiences of women and, perhaps above all, a group structure which encourages participation of all members in the connecting up of our everyday struggles with the search for God has had a healing and encouraging impact on my growth as a person, and on my sense of living out a part of the story of God in my own life. It has been necessary to create Womanchurch because an essential part of our silencing in the Church comes with the all-pervading use of androcentric language in the liturgy. While grace and liberation have been experienced in the everyday lives of women attending Church there has been little outlet for expressing in church the feminine face of God. The self-doubt which does not easily speak out its visions has been one result, as Elisabeth Schüssler Fiorenza describes:

> Do women belong to the 'Family of men' and do we share in
> the 'spirit of brotherhood'? Not only are men or humans 'he',
> but so also is God 'Himself' in whose image we are made.
> Women do not figure in the language about divine reality and
> in the theological articulation of the 'world'.
>
> (Schüssler Fiorenza, 1993)

While waiting for ordination to the priesthood we have found places to figure, places to practise our priesthood in the creation of healing and celebratory rituals, places to be released out of anger into creativity.

Womanchurch was born in America in 1977 and held its first

large meeting in 1983. That meeting declared that 'Women are Church', that to be a community of redemption *is* to be Church. Rosemary Ruether declared 'Women engaged in liberation from patriarchy declare this community of women's liberation to be theologically, church, that is to say, a community of redemption' (Ruether, 1985).

There are different models of Womanchurch flourishing in many parts of the world. Mary Grey describes three. She describes the Women and Faith Movement in the Netherlands where Womanchurch has developed from political struggle on a national level around issues such as incest, sexual violence and poverty. She describes one American model, Women's Association for Theology, Ethics and Ritual, in which friends meet around a common quest for justice for women and marginalized groups, finding ritual expression for their hopes and beliefs. She describes, too, the movements in England, from Women in Theology and the Catholic Women's Network, with their commitment to the development of ritual and the struggle for justice, to the St Hilda Community, struggling to give inclusivity and mutuality expression in worship, to the Movement for the Ordination of Women in the Church of England, with its declaration that Womanchurch cannot remain marginal, that the insights, gifts and ministry of women matter for the whole Church (Grey, 1993, pp. 123–7).

Many of us have belonged to branches of these English groups or have attended small feminist meetings of a house group type. I belonged to Chloe's People, in Bristol, where Chloe stood for 'Creative Happenings, Liturgy and Other Events'. There our aim was small. It was to create liturgies using inclusive language and to support each other in friendship. But the impact of that small and faltering group on my life was enormous! For I experienced the full reality of the talent of women in the making of meaningful liturgy, and felt for myself the gap which exists between the experience of Sunday morning church and the possibilities within people for making liturgy part of life and life-enhancing. I realized as never before we are wasting the visions of vast numbers of women and men in the hours spent sitting in rigid rows, singing Victorian hymns containing outdated theology and watching other people perform at the front.

Part of the silence concerning a future vision of priesthood of any deacon who has been part of such a group lies in the daunting knowledge that our language, hymnody, teaching methods and lack of enablement of lay people to stand up and be supported in their Christian vision is not merciful. Even in our most flourishing churches we have an actor and spectator style which is weakening the chance for lay people to tell their own story of faith and doubt and to be re-created by that telling. The quality of mercy to be expected of us as priests is that we should be merciful, not in a patronizing 'doing good to others who are evidently needy' way, but in an enablement of others to be fully themselves as loved by God. Being merciful includes allowing the strengths of others to be seen, and being able to receive from that strength.

It is difficult to speak clearly of a vision of a more participatory Church when the language of that Church has so silenced us in the past. Many of us have grown by managing to maintain one foot in and one foot outside of the structures. Part of our silence is due to a fear that ordination to the priesthood means two feet in, when it was standing on the one foot out which allowed us to grow in our vision of ourselves as being fully acceptable to God, and made creative in God's image.

A third reason for maintaining a trembling silence as we contemplate the future is that we fear being compromised, becoming people with power over others and divided from each other as women. Dorothee Sölle, in *Thinking about God*, describes the gap between the understanding of divine authority in conservative theology and the understanding of divine authority in feminist and liberation theologies:

> The appeal to God is ambiguous, and the weakness of conservative theology is that it points to God only assertively ('But our God is the right one'), only theoretically. The basis of faith is not that it was Christ who spoke with divine authority; the basis of faith is the praxis of the poor man from Nazareth who shared his bread with the hungry, made the blind see, and lived and died for justice.
>
> (Sölle, 1990)

Women deacons have known some solidarity with each other

and with others throughout the world who have been judged and found wanting not on account of their gifts and abilities but on account of their gender, race, class, creed, income, sexual orientation or colour. They have been hurt by men who have said 'God is like this. Therefore you cannot be that.' They have been forced to live in exodus, always on the way, always finding God walking alongside each other, never being allowed to be out in front. While not perfect in our companionship we have nevertheless been forced to know something of Elisabeth Schüssler Fiorenza's vision of Church as a 'Discipleship of Equals' (Schüssler Fiorenza, 1993, p. 237). As such a group of disciples we have not felt ill at ease with groups of secular feminists, and have been welcomed as people of protest in the women's movement.

It is understandable that we should now fear assimilation into the masculine structures and ways of being with each other which are characteristic in the Church. Two examples may serve to highlight this fear. Beverly Alimo-Metcalfe in her work 'Gender, leadership, and assessment' (Alimo-Metcalfe, 1990) shows how research undertaken in the US in the 1970s revealed that the qualities expected of successful middle managers were closely aligned by both men and women with qualities they ascribed not to women in general but to men in general. In 1989 the research was repeated with depressing results. While women's perceptions of the characteristics of women in general were more highly correlated with their perceptions of the qualities of successful managers, nothing had changed with respect to the male managers' perceptions of women in general and their perceptions of successful middle managers. Alimo-Metcalfe proceeds to demonstrate how male role definitions influence both interview and ongoing assessment procedures so that it is difficult for women to speak with their own voice and to alter the nature of the organizations in which they work. This research suggests that women entering the Church as priests have good reason to fear whether they will be able to change the system sufficiently to feel at home within it.

The second example lies in my own recent experience and demonstrates our fear that, as women deacons, we shall lose solidarity with each other. I belong to a small support group for women deacons which meets once a month. Early last year some

of us met to plan a large service of celebration for the successful
outcome of the vote in November. Group cohesiveness fell apart
before our eyes as one declared a need to work quickly in creating
a form of service, while another was more used to liturgy being
created slowly and meditatively from the group's wrestling with
a theme. One wanted vestments worn while another didn't want
the same old distinctions between clergy and lay people perpetu-
ated. One wanted a simple celebration, unthreatening in its style
or theology; another wanted an expression of solidarity with
feminists everywhere. The experience was both funny and shat-
tering. We shall not achieve sameness with each other simply by
becoming priests, and we shall have lost the cohesion created
by being viewed by others as an opposition. It will take time and
work to learn how to support each other and to find a strong
non-competitive voice. We shall need more than deanery chapter
meetings to prevent us from splitting away from each other and
becoming individual priests with our own agenda of isolation
and competition. To break down long-established patriarchalist
theologies and hierarchical structures in the Church we shall
need to learn how to speak with a common voice. Otherwise we
risk simply becoming honorary members of a male club, powerless and voiceless once more, mimics of the 'Looking Glass
Priests' described by Virginia Woolf.

Finding the strength of a shared voice will be new to us, and
difficult, but not impossible. I found my own voice working in a
psychiatric hospital, but it was in another work context that I
discovered a model for how that voice could be both distinct *and*
quiet enough to hear the voices of others.

After working as a social worker with children and families
for several years I took my new skills into the different context
of a paediatric renal unit. I was very drawn to this post because
the young renal consultant, who was a woman, had established
a pattern for discussing the psycho-social needs of the young
patients collectively.

Each week a multi-disciplinary team met to exchange news
and ideas concerning therapeutic possibilities for the children and
their families. I was excited by the team approach and talked
often with other social workers, whose consultants did not use
team discussion methods, of what a difference such an innovation

made to a young person's experience of chronic illness. This seemed to be a good example of one simple action breaking down rigid boundaries of hierarchy, or at least of initiating that process of change.

Learning to work in a team was, however, shockingly difficult. Field social work requires that a social worker be advocate, welfare rights adviser, play therapist, couples counsellor, in addition to car driver, note-taker and court report writer. Nothing had prepared me to diminish my own voice to make one contribution alongside the contribution of others. I wanted to do everything and to do it well! My lack of popularity and usefulness as a team member mystified me until I learned how painful it was for others that I should usurp their role, perhaps taking over some aspect of work which they had been doing well enough for years. I learned to watch the gaps, to find out what was not being done and why. I learned, particularly, that if a dietician, nurse or play worker possessed skill in being alongside a certain family, it was that skill which needed supporting rather than challenging. I learned that to be part of a team is to acknowledge one's complete ineptitude in some situations and to let others take over, enjoying their voice. I learned that simply to discover one's own voice is not enough because the lone voice can be merciless.

No story better illustrates what I learned there than the story of Colin [another pseudonym], which is a story of passivity in the midst of activity, of silence in the midst of noise.

Behind the colourful clatter of the life of a paediatric ward there lies a painful silence. The silence becomes palpable when a whole team waits for figures to come back from a laboratory indicating whether a new medicine is taking effect or not. It becomes heavy when a family sits around a bed in intensive care, waiting for signs of life, or the news of death. The silence is about the future of each child; it is about human powerlessness in the face of immense suffering; it is about the mystery at the very heart of life—why this child, why this family, why is life so wonderful, so painful, so fragile?

One early reaction to this silence is to break it, to blow up the balloon to cheer the child, to exchange words of planning with a colleague, to reassure parents, to switch on a machine and monitor its workings in minute detail, to fill out forms, to turn back the bed, to check the administration of drugs, to speak, to act, to do. Around each ill child a whole team dances in activity.

Such activity is both necessary and merciful. No child is likely to improve in health dismally contemplating her fate with no diversion. Her family need to feel aware that they are at the very centre of a series of carefully planned and skilfully executed actions, that a concerted effort is being made by a trusted group of people to stem the progress of the illness and to comfort the child. The garden full of brightly coloured play equipment which I passed on my way to work each morning was as important as the operating theatre, for it summoned the child towards the goal of everyone's work, the enjoyment of her own good health.

Yet it was easy for such work to become unorchestrated, for staff members to conceal hopelessness in the face of illness and death by becoming over-busy, over-intent on doing, competitive with each other for the child's ear, the family's appreciation. Avoiding the silence at the heart of the matter, which needed to be faced, we sometimes fell over each other, demanding that problems be solved, anxiety be alleviated, the pain of human living be swept off the corridors of the ward at the end of the day as easily as toys into a box. I discovered that my most difficult task was to face the silence, to learn how to do nothing, to wait and give space to those who needed to act, to watch long enough to know what it was necessary to do, and no more. Much of this I learned from being involved with Colin and his family.

Colin suffered both kidney disease and disease of the bone marrow. He had an adult brother who was well, but had lost a sister suffering the same rare condition. He himself faced renal replacement therapy, to be followed by a renal transplant, and either a bone–marrow transplant or prolonged chemotherapy. He was little more than a baby when he first came to us and by the age of three was attached at home overnight to a machine which assisted dialysis in paediatric renal patients.

The tasks which faced Colin's parents every day for the next few years appeared insurmountable, even without the need to continue earning a living. When Colin's machine 'alarmed' at night, the parents had to attend to it immediately, and this machine 'alarmed' sometimes, broke down mysteriously at other times. Nights were broken. Days were often spent in driving over 100 miles with an ill child in the car to the hospital. Colin was fed through a naso-gastric tube, frequently felt tired, and displayed the imperious behaviour of a child who seemed to know how vital to his life was the zealous care and good-humoured presence of his mother. Much loved on the ward, he was understandably demanding in his family circle. While he enjoyed play, his mother ruefully and stoically accepted that he could not be left for very long to play with others, that she must be his main companion over the next few years.

At times, anxiety within the team rose to fever pitch over Colin. His machine had broken down again; he was not gaining weight; he was regressing in his behaviour; the local medical staff were furious over not receiving from us the latest care-plan; his mother was looking grey with tiredness; how could anyone ever persuade this gentle, determined woman to talk of all that had beset her? How much longer could she hold on? How much longer could we all go on without seeing signs of improvement? What was the future? Was it all worthwhile? What quality of life did Colin have?

What I learned from that family was that there was very little that I could do in any active sense. The dedicated activity lay with them, with the medical and nursing staff and, increasingly, with Colin's nursery staff and school staff. It also lay with him. It was his task to keep going, to keep asking for what he wanted, to keep attempting to go to nursery, to keep trying at his school work. This was not the time for 'counselling', whether about the past or the future. The past was being redeemed and the future being made in Colin's daily life. I filled in forms, liaised with local caring agencies and drove down from time to time to keep in touch. These trips I thoroughly enjoyed because I was fond of the family, but I rarely wanted to add to the enormous stream of professionals entering that home. For me it was a time for silence, for watching from afar, for attending quietly to the drama which had become centre-stage in this family's life.

When I last *saw* Colin he was using his own voice, a mixture of bashfulness and cheek, to welcome a member of the royal family who was visiting the hospital. When I last *heard news* of Colin he had survived a renal transplant and was settling into school enjoying both the work and new-found friends!

As I worked out my role in relation to Colin and the other patients I discovered that I could only be a strong member of a multi-disciplinary team by being rooted in my identity in the social work department of the hospital. It was there that I was accepted as anxious, moody and rude, as well as competent, playful and laughing. If we are insecure in our own voice, not gaining support and challenge in a place of primary belonging, it is very difficult to yield up power to others in places of greater threat.

I had learned to share the undersong, not to attempt to sing it on my own.

If as women deacons becoming priests we hope to sing an undersong of mercy then we shall need to take time together, to meet regularly to listen to each other, and support each other. For where clergy neither accept nor respect each other there is a danger that we strive to gain control over the people among whom we work, not secure enough in ourselves to enable them to find their voice. The priestly community is then disempowered by its ordained ministers. Far from losing our anger or our vulnerability at ordination, together we must take our anger and our vulnerability into our priesthood, so that we may stay close to the energy and pain of the world, and allow ourselves to be close to its rich variety of people and to each other. If holiness is to be shared by the priesthood of all believers, if we are to develop in such a way as to empower the Church, and not deskill its laity, then we shall have to be willing to bear such interdependence.

When I think of our voicelessness being past, as this book of essays signifies, and of the beginning of singing, I think of the image of music supporting life which Primo Levi threads through his novel *If Not Now, When?* (Levi, 1987). The novel pays tribute to the Jews who fought back during the holocaust. It is a tale of unimaginable hardship, of cold, pain, terror, hunger and weariness, of exile in marshes and forests, sewers, caves and collapsed buildings where Russian and Polish refugees, stranded in occupied territory, resist the German army. Their suffering was so great, and the intention behind their persecution so evil, that I wish to make no comparison between my own story and that group's history. But I am drawn, for an image of my priesthood, to the picture of their lone violinist, who plays throughout the group's adventures, crises and moral struggles. Faithful to his calling, he plays for a mock wedding. He plays when strength is gone in the snow, forcing people to stamp their feet to keep alive. He plays and sings to restore the group's memory of its history. At times the very reason to live is contained in the playing. Yet the playing is to enable the group to dance. Such dancing inspires the violinist himself to join in, so that he too is part of the group's celebration when the war is over.

> Gedaleh, seated in a corner of the car, his back against the wooden wall, was playing in his fashion, softly, absently. He was playing a zigeuner tune, or Jewish, or Russian: a humble tune, heard a hundred times, commonplace, cheap, nostalgic: and then, suddenly, the rhythm turned fast: and the tune, accelerated in this easy way, became something else: lively, new, noble, filled with hope. A dancing happy rhythm that invited you to follow it, swaying your head and clapping your hands. The traps were over, the war was over, the way, the blood and ice: the satan of Berlin was dead, the world was empty and vacant, to be recreated, repopulated, like after the Flood. The violinist, too, had risen to his feet, and was dancing as he played . . .
>
> (Levi, 1987, p. 254)

The rhythm is turning fast for us, the tune is being accelerated. As we sing the undersong which we have known for so long may we, delivered of our own voicelessness, remember that it is an undersong of mercy for the dancing of the world. For Gedaleh was able also to be silent. At the group's first party he had followed Pavel the mimic, Mottel the fire-thrower, Bella the singer, Dov the story-teller, Lionid and Piotr the wrestlers. Indeed the evening was growing late when he began to play: 'Some were already sleeping when Gedaleh took up his violin and began to sing; but he wasn't singing for applause. He sang softly, he who was so loud when he spoke' (Levi, 1987, p. 127).

My vision of priesthood is this—to achieve such silence and such singing within communities of endurance and hope.

References

B. Alimo-Metcalfe, 'Gender, leadership and assessment', adapted from a paper presented to the Third European Congress on the Assessment Centre Method, Geneval-Les-Eaux, Belgium, 28–30 November 1990, to be published in *Management Assessment* (Whitbread—in press).

L. M. Brown and C. Gilligan, 'Meeting at the crossroads: women's psychology and girls' development', *Feminism and Psychology* 3.1 (February 1993), pp. 11–89.

A. V. Campbell, *The Gospel of Anger* (London: SPCK, 1986), p. 14.

M. Daly, *Beyond God the Father* (London: The Women's Press, 1986), p. 195.

M. Grey, *The Wisdom of Fools?* (London: SPCK, 1993), p. 110.

G. Herbert, 'Bitter Sweet' in H. Gardner (ed.), *The Faber Book of Religious Verse* (London: Faber and Faber, 1972), p. 129.

P. Levi, *If Not Now, When?* (London: Sphere Books, 1987).

T. P. McDonnell, *A Thomas Merton Reader* (London: Lamp Press, 1989), p. 351.

A. Nye, *Words of Power* (London: Routledge, 1990).

R. Ruether in M. J. Weaver, *New Catholic Women: A Contemporary Challenge to Traditional Religious Authority* (San Francisco: Harper and Row, 1985), p. 133.

E. Schüssler Fiorenza, *Discipleship of Equals* (London: SCM, 1993), p. 264.

D. Sölle, *Thinking About God* (London: SCM, 1990), p. 19.

4

Vision for the future: the symbol of woman

The opportunity and challenge of the ordination of women in the Church of England

CATHY MILFORD

The long wait

It ought, of course, to have been very easy to ordain women to the priesthood in the Church of England. A quiet revolution has gone on in the last thirty years. Half of those now studying theology or religious studies in our colleges and universities are women; a third of those now selected and trained in Church of England theological colleges and ministerial training courses are women; women have been made deacon alongside their male peers for some years, and, for the most part, have had very similar experiences as they served their titles. Many women deacons have borne moving witness to their recognition that their own ministry is priestly as they have discovered its profound depths. In truth, the question has become no longer, 'The priesthood ... a woman's place?' but 'The priesthood ... a *woman's* place'.

This has been backed up at a practical level. The Church of England is now short of parish priests. To ordain women as priests will go some way to making up the shortfall. Admittedly we cannot at the moment pay for all the parish priests we need, the balance between the numbers of stipendiary and honorary parish priests needed in the future has yet to be worked out, as has the proper role of the laity in the parish, but it may well be that women have a major part to play in the reshaping of styles of parish ministry in the future. This is a very exciting prospect. Women may bring the necessary gifts of community building, networking and sharing that are required for this reshaping of ministry.

Why then has it been so hard to move ahead? The short answer can only be that we are not reasonable people, we are unreasonable people. It is precisely in the long delay that we have uncovered some of the hidden depths of our own unreasonableness. Feelings still run high and are very murky on both sides of the divide. It is not just that there is a deep revulsion against women as priests on the side of those who have bitterly opposed the decision; it is that there is an inherent revulsion in our traditional structures. By way of example I point to the first draft of *The Bishops' Code of Practice* (1990) drawn up as a guideline to the implementation of the legislation to ordain women as priests.

> Bishops will seek themselves, and will encourage others, to be sensitive in making arrangements for diocesan, archdeaconry and deanery services in circumstances where women priests serve in the area but there are also significant numbers who find the exercise of priestly functions by a woman unacceptable. Where this latter position is known to be predominant it would be inappropriate for a woman priest to exercise those priestly functions; in other cases the identity of the officiant should be made known in advance.
>
> (para. 18, The House of Bishops' Draft Code of Practice, *GS Misc.* 336, p. 39)

Only substitute the words 'non-Aryan priests' for 'women priests' and the blatant prejudice is immediately recognizable. Not surprisingly women cried out in rage and asked for this paragraph to be redrafted. In our country we may still think along such sexist lines but we are no longer allowed to enshrine such thoughts in codes of practice. Such is the depth of the traditional revulsion against women in the structure of the Church that this draft of the Code of Practice has not been redrafted; it still stands. Yet the majority of bishops in the Church of England are strongly in favour of the ordination of women. They are friends of the movement and they have worked hard at the management of the legislation. In spite of this they, or their legal advisers, have colluded with this age-old revulsion towards women, regarding it as a necessary part of the prolonged process of our reception into the structures of the Church.

There are other murky depths. It is easy to point to the hysterical rage of some of those who oppose the movement and to allow all the blame to be projected onto them. It is less easy to confront our own rage. The age-old story of Jane and Abel:

> Now Abel was a deacon and kept watch over the flock, while Jane was a deacon and worked hard for food for the flock. In the course of time Jane brought to the Lord an offering of her labours, and Abel for his part brought an offering of his labour. And the Lord had regard for Abel and his offering, but for Jane and her offering he had no regard. So Jane was very angry and her countenance fell. The Lord said to Jane 'Why are you angry, and why has your countenance fallen? If you do well, will you not be accepted? And if you do not well, sin is lurking at the door; its desire is for you, but you must master it.' Jane said to her brother Abel, 'Let us go out to the churchyard'. And when they were in the churchyard, Jane rose up against her brother Abel, and killed him with her stiletto.
>
> (Genesis 4.2–8 NRSV, adapted by the writer)

We deal indeed with murky depths and it may be that much of the exhaustion of women working for the Church is that we are struggling with 'sin lurking at the door and its desire for us'. It is very difficult to confront the structures without hitting back very hard at individuals when murk is thrown our way. The Church of England has long used fagging or bullying as a method of institutional control. In the past, male curates have colluded because their escape route to incumbencies has been built into the system. The good thing today is that women are learning to confront the ugly face of the structure because they have been trapped within it as parish workers and assistant curates for a long stretch of time. This confrontation can only be of long-term benefit to the institution.

The irony in the Genesis story comes in God's question to Jane: 'Will you not be accepted?' The irony is the more because the repeated theme of our Bible is that God lifts up the countenance of the lowly and the rejected. God lifts up the *anawim*, the bent-over ones, and therefore the story that holds our hope is

the story of Jesus making whole the bent-over woman in the
synagogue, dare I say Church.

> Now Jesus was teaching in one of the churches on Sunday. And
> just then there appeared a woman with a spirit that had
> crippled her for eighteen years. She was bent over and was quite
> unable to stand up straight. When Jesus saw her, he called her
> over and said, 'Woman, you are set free from your ailment'.
> When he laid hands on her, immediately she stood up straight
> and began praising God . . . And Jesus said, 'Ought not this
> woman, a daughter of God whom Satan bound for eighteen
> long years, be set free from this bondage on a Sunday?'
> (Luke 13.10–16 NRSV, adapted by the writer)

Because we often fail to ask the question a Hebrew person would
ask, 'What does this story mean?', we fail also to recognize the
richness of the symbolism in the story. The children of Israel
gave thanks to God standing upright with their arms lifted to
heaven. We know this in theory, as this is what is intended in
the Rite A Eucharistic Prayer in the Alternative Service Book.
So the bent-over woman could not give thanks to God. Notice
Jesus says she was bound by Satan. Notice that he said 'Ought
not this woman be set free on a Sunday?'

The challenge to us today is to continue the process of untying
the bonds of Satan that have kept women bent over in the
Church for eighteen long centuries, untying them now at last on
the Sunday so that they may stand up straight, praise God and
make eucharist.

This challenge is required by God's justice, by God's shalom
and by the prayer 'Your Kingdom come'. The General Synod
report *And All That Is Unseen* (1986) makes it clear that women
bear the brunt of the world's poverty and powerlessness. If the
Church is to speak out in God's name on vital issues of justice
in the world today we must continue to do all that is necessary
to remove the plank that is in our own eye.

The positive outcome of the long wait

Fortunately, there has been a positive side to the unreasonable
delay to remove this injustice to women. First, the issues have
been laid out in the open, and when issues are out in the open

healing has already begun. Second, in a very real sense those
who have laboured long for the delay have been unwise. They
have allowed the opening of a veritable treasure trove of exciting
insights and possibilities. Peter Selby put it like this in his talk
at the Southwark MOW AGM in 1991:

> Just think what might have happened if the Church of England
> had replied to the first woman who felt called to ordination,
> 'Great, go and get yourself selected, trained and ordained'. If
> that had happened we might never have heard about inclusive
> language, non-hierarchical concepts of authority and about new
> ways of pastoring.

Come to that, what would have happened if the Church had
replied 'Great, when it says man in the Ordinal of the Book of
Common Prayer man includes women, so go ahead'?

So the delayers have been the losers and the waiters have been
the gainers, gainers in that they have been able to discover and
articulate that which lies beneath the surface of the struggle to
ordain women as priests. The flowering of feminist theology,
feminist spirituality and feminist liturgy bears this out. Publishing houses would not publish the feminist books that they do if
it did not pay them to do so. The Archbishop of Canterbury
had only to issue a warning that the St Hilda's liturgies are not
authorized for public use in the Church of England for *Women
Included* (1991) to go into its third printing.

I have been forcibly struck by Janet Morley's Advent prayer
in *Bread of Tomorrow* (1992):

> You keep us waiting.
> You, the God of all time,
> want us to wait
> for the right time in which to discover
> who we are, where we must go,
> who will be with us, and what we must do.
> So thank you ... for the waiting time.
>
> (p. 15)

In the long wait for the ordination of women there has been
much gain. Those who oppose the ordination of women to the
priesthood are right at one very important level: what is required
by the priesting of women is a transformation of our ways of

perceiving, feeling and thinking, and ultimately nothing less than a transformation of our church structures. Although this will not happen overnight, what is required is a conversion. The priesting of women is not a simple, rational, legal matter; it is a challenge to repentance and conversion. The question is, will this challenge be accepted and will the risk be taken to discover a new way of working within the church community for the sake of the Kingdom?

The revaluing of the feminine

The challenge and the opportunity of this new order lies in our rediscovery of, and our revaluing of, the feminine heart of the tradition and the feminine heart of God.

Much excitement and energy has come from the reclaiming and revaluing of the place of women in the biblical story, from the discovery of the voices of Eve, Sarah, Hagar, Jochebed, Miriam, Puah and Shiphrah and Pharaoh's daughter, to name only some of the women's stories as they are retold by Trevor Dennis (1994); through to the rediscovery of the part played by the women round Jesus by Elisabeth Moltmann-Wendel (1980). The same reclamation and revaluing of the part played by women in the Church story has also taken place.

The rediscovery and revaluing of the feminine heart of the Bible and the tradition has had the knock-on effect of the rediscovery and revaluing of the feminine heart of God. Much work is being done by women theologians such as Mary Tanner, Angela Tilby and Sarah Coakley, work which begins to bear fruit in the Church of Scotland's report *The Motherhood of God* (1984) and the Doctrine Commission's report *We Believe in the Holy Spirit* (1991).

Another significant change has been experienced by many people in the use of language and imagery in worship, both in the description of the created order and in the description of God. It is no accident that the Churches which have already accepted the priesting of women have made a dramatic move in the use of language and imagery in their liturgy. The Church of New Zealand, the Iona Community, the United Reformed

Church and the Methodist Church all bear this out. Jim Cotter's
Lord's Prayer (1983) bears striking testimony to this:

> Eternal Spirit,
> Earth-maker, Pain-bearer, Life-giver,
> Source of all that is and that shall be,
> Father and Mother of us all,
> Loving God, in whom is heaven:
>
> (p. 42)

We are not helped in all this by the way in which we use the
words feminine and masculine because we almost inevitably
equate the words feminine and masculine with female and male.
We should not, but we do. In our society we ascribe the nurturing
and community-building characteristics to the feminine and the
challenging and ordering characteristics to the masculine, hence,
no doubt, 'Orders' in the Church.

Now many men are good nurturers and community builders
and many women are good challengers and organizers. Both
individuals and society require a balance of both characteristics;
gender is not a guide to their possession. Jesus embodied both
the ability to nurture and build community and the ability to
challenge and order. The biblical story tells of God as both a
God of compassion, who brings life forth from the womb and
builds a community of people, and a God of challenge and order.
God both is in disorder and chaos and brings order out of chaos.
It is a question of balance and of the appropriateness of the
response at any given moment. Our western society has for long
had an imbalance in its valuation of these characteristics and the
masculine has been predominant.

Mary Tanner (1986) writes:

> As we learn to celebrate the feminine in God as well as the
> masculine, we re-value the feminine in human life. This brings
> healing not only for women, but enables men to value their
> femininity and in so doing allows women to discover the repressed
> masculinity within themselves. And so integration within each
> one of us is supported, as well as between women and men,
> by our view of God.
>
> (p. 10)

The importance of the revaluation of the feminine

Why is all this important? It seems that the revaluing of the feminine is important not for the sake of the Church but for the sake of the world. I often wonder why the press has been so interested in the issue of the ordination of women. Partly no doubt because of malicious delight in seeing a once powerful institution threatening to implode. But I suspect it is more than that. The press must sense that the Church has been publicly playing out something on behalf of society, throwing images up on a screen for all to see. And I am not afraid of that, because I believe that part of the Church's task is to image and articulate that which is of importance to society. We often think that the Church speaks 'to' society; my guess is that the Church actually speaks 'for' society. The Church is one of the articulators, interpreters, speaking trumpets, for the underlying dynamics of society. When we are in touch with that reality we are perhaps doing our job. We have been joined by the press, and not always helped by them, but at least they recognize our common task. Angela Tilby (1992) writes:

> A church which has inherited and seeks to sustain close
> connections with the identity of the nation has to be competent
> in its dealings with the mass media, which link together all
> those facets of social life which make up 'the national parish'.
> TV lives, exactly as does the church, by a series of interactions.
> The two are also joined through a concern for communication.
> This is the heart of gospel. The ability to communicate is
> expressed and reaffirmed in every liturgical act.
> Communication involves dialogue. And there is a prophetic and
> priestly dimension. With this few would argue. Yet it is often
> overlooked that at this juncture all media work parallels the life
> of the church, because it has to do with the transmission of
> words and images, which is a sacred task.
>
> (p. 82)

We are image-making and symbol-using people. We use images and symbols to communicate with each other and to communicate with God. Without images and symbols we would be handicapped and impoverished. In our western society woman has become the symbol of nurture and community, the symbol of the feminine. I said before that I believed that both women and

men carry both feminine and masculine characteristics and that
to be fully human is to be able to use the full range of these
characteristics. Having said that, within our society woman is the
symbol of the feminine, and it seems to me that what is happening is that our society badly needs to recover the feminine and
that need has actually triggered the search and the revaluation
in the Church. The movement in the Church is part of a much
wider movement. If the Church is to communicate with society
the Church must also revalue the feminine. The way it can
symbolize this best is through ordination, allowing women to
take on the representative role of the priest; allowing women into
the heart of the structure. Now that this has at last happened
we have to face the risk of the disappointment that women also
will fail to glory in the power that is love. The opportunity which
opens out before us is that women and men together may now
find a new way of symbolizing the community life of which we
are now so much in need.

I have suggested that the symbols we use matter very much
indeed because they form our value systems. Consider the symbols of our present western culture. We give glory and honour
and power to wealth and success. More hidden, more subtle, we
give glory and honour and blessing to military might. We do not
like to admit it, it is one of our best kept secrets, but we do. In
the Church we do not like to admit that we worship the 'Lord
God of the armies', but we do. Rite A in the Alternative Service
Book disguises the words as 'God of power and might'. The Book
of Common Prayer is more open, 'God of Sabaoth', but how
many who sing the Sanctus week by week know that the word
Sabaoth means 'of the armies'? Just why do some people object
to Janet Morley's Sanctus (1992): 'Holy, Holy, Holy, Vulnerable
God'?

With my family I spent some years in Uganda and I remember
vividly the time when General Amin turned sour and civil war
began. The men went to war. You could feel the women bending
over to take up the heavy burden of the struggle to survive. They
did not prevent the men from going to war. Were they powerless?
Did they collude? How can you prevent the use of guns? I have
stood myself at the wrong end of one of Amin's army guns. That
was enough to let me know where overt power lies.

I found myself in the shoes of the Ugandan women during the Gulf War. Was I powerless? Did I collude? What could I do to stop people with guns? That seems to be one of the basic human questions. 'How, Madam', asked the sixth-form students in Uganda, 'how do you keep the army out of power in England?' I had no answer to give them then, and now I know that I had no answer then because, in a much more subtle way, we also have a military society in England. The Gulf crisis revealed to those who had eyes to see the abyss on which humanity stands. The tools for deadly precision bombing are the design of a military society, and I say society advisedly because I do not wish to indict individuals. Our society and our history have been shaped by military societies from time immemorial. From the horsemen of the steppes, to the armies of the Romans, to the military structures of our own Northmen or Viking culture.

In our culture the symbol of cherishing has been woman. This has contributed much that is vital to society because we know that cherishing in the early days of life is the key to maturity. But there is a difficulty. For centuries this symbol of cherishing has been pushed into the private arena of the household, sidelined by the masculine symbol of power which dominated the public domain.

I do believe that now there is a universal struggle to redress the balance and that a shift may begin to take place in our archetypes and symbols. Women have begun to come out of the private arena and play their part in the public domain. Women have begun to play a part in public decision-making processes. I say begun advisedly, for it is fraught with difficulty. Aung San Suu Kyi is a symbol for our time. The elected leader of her country, yet under house arrest in Burma, she stands as a challenge to the military powers of that country and offers an alternative, a society based on generosity and compassion.

I do believe that the qualities which we in the West have chosen to call feminine are now desperately needed in the public domain of our world—compassion, nurture, grace, generosity, charity, vulnerability, community building, all these—and they are also qualities of God.

Michael Berkeley (1984), in his operetta *Or Shall We Die?*, puts this very poignantly:

> Shall there be womanly times, or shall we die?
> Are there men unafraid of gentleness?
> Can we have strength without aggression,
> without disgust,
> strength to bind feeling to the intellect?
>
> The planet does not turn for us alone.
> Science is a form of wonder,
> knowledge a form of love.
> Are we too late to love ourselves?
> Shall we change or shall we die?
> Shall there be womanly times, or shall we die?

The planet does not turn for us alone

The planet does not turn for us alone and many are the prophetic voices that have warned of that for the last half century. We need also to cherish our planet earth, Gaia, of whom we are an integral part.

It is interesting that the reclamation and revaluing that we are engaged upon world wide is interwoven with reclaiming and revaluing the cherishing images from primal societies: the Primal Vision in Africa of which Bishop John Taylor (1970) has written so tellingly; the struggle of the indigenous people in Latin America; our own Celtic vision, where God is to be found in all things, and all things are sacramental; the heritage of the indigenous peoples of New Zealand and Canada where all are included in the circle. The Wild Goose of Iona would find itself at home with the Snow Goose of the Native Americans in Canada.

And what of the roots of our own biblical heritage? If we are intent on transformation, on radical change, we have only to reclaim our own roots. Within the Bible is held the belief that 'The earth is the Lord's and all that therein is', and that we are but stewards. It is perhaps the gospel of John which has grasped some of this. Odd, or not odd, that John is the gospel that hovers on the edge of being marginalized by the Church. Alan Ecclestone (1987) reminds us in his book *The Scaffolding of Spirit* that 'Almost alone amongst first-century Christian writing, John points to the part which womanhood must occupy in the reshaping of human life which metaphorically is called being born again' (p. 64).

If womanhood is to play that part, then the Church as well as the secular world must allow the re-imaging of symbols. Hugh Montefiore (1972) points to the profound importance of symbols in the Eucharist itself:

> One image leads to another: images become fused . . .
> . . . it is through the images and symbolic actions of the
> eucharist that people are able to pay attention to God in Christ:
> and it is part of the God-given structure of the rite that natural
> images are given religious overtones and associations. A change
> of emphasis through symbolic action (such as standing in a
> circle to receive communion, or laying the table at the
> offertory) can re-orientate the rite far more than an alteration
> in the wording of an eucharistic prayer.
>
> (pp. 77, 79)

The image of the male priest at the altar has been internalized for so long in the Church that the re-imaging required by the priesting of women is fraught with anxiety, as well as being a longed-for sign of hope. Yet the re-imaging must take place if Church and society are to be reshaped.

Is it a coincidence that the conditions of our time are calling for the re-imaging of woman and man? Or is this now desperately needed by our society and by the planet earth? The Church is caught up in this universal struggle. The transformation of our images and symbols which the priesting of women entails is part of a much wider whole. Are we at last catching some insights into the feminine heart of God, who longs for us to share in the vision of a future which is different? If so, the struggle for the symbol of women and men working together as priests for the sake of the Kingdom will not have been in vain.

References

Michael Berkeley, *Or Shall We Die?* (Oxford University Press, 1984).
Jim Cotter, *Prayer at Night* (Cairns Publications, 1983), p. 42.
Rosemary Dawson (ed.), *And All That Is Unseen: A New Look at Women and Work* (Industrial and Economic Affairs Committee of

the General Synod Board for Social Responsibility; Church House
Publishing, 1986).

Trevor Dennis, *Sarah Laughed: Women's Voices in the Old Testament*
(SPCK, 1994).

Doctrine Commission, *We Believe in the Holy Spirit: A Report of
the Doctrine Commission of The Church of England* (Church House
Publishing, 1991).

Alan Ecclestone, *The Scaffolding of Spirit* (Darton, Longman & Todd,
1987), p. 64.

House of Bishops, *Reference of Draft Legislation to the Diocesan Synods
1990: Memorandum by the Standing Committee and Background
Papers, GS Misc.* 336 (Church House Publishing, 1990), p. 39.

Alan Lewis (ed.), *The Motherhood of God: Report of the Women's Guild
Panel on Doctrine Study Group* (St Andrew Press, 1984).

Elisabeth Moltmann-Wendel, *The Women Around Jesus* (Crossroad,
1980).

Hugh Montefiore, 'Symbols and the eucharist' in *Thinking About the
Eucharist: Papers by Members of the Church of England Doctrine
Commission* (SCM, 1972), pp. 77, 79.

Janet Morley, *All Desires Known* (SPCK, 1992), p. 46.

Janet Morley (ed.), *Bread of Tomorrow* (SPCK/Christian Aid, 1992),
p. 15.

The St Hilda Community, *Women Included: A Book of Services and
Prayers* (SPCK, 1991).

Mary Tanner, *Christian Feminism: A Challenge to the Churches* (Annual
Lecture to Loughborough University and Colleges Anglican Chap-
laincy; Loughborough: Quorn Selective Repro Ltd, 1986).

John V. Taylor, *The Primal Vision* (SCM, 1963).

Angela Tilby, 'Alternative images' in Wesley Carr (ed.), *Say One For
Me* (SPCK, 1992), p. 82.

5

Renewing the place

CHRISTINE FARRINGTON

My love–hate relationship with the Church of England began over 35 years ago when I discovered with a shock that although God might be calling women to ministry, the Church appeared stubbornly deaf to the possibility of allowing those vocations to be tested and fulfilled. It was right and fitting for women to teach in Sunday school, arrange flowers, make coffee, clean the church, but the sanctuary and all aspects of sacramental ministry were to be reserved for the male of the species only. It made no sense to me then, in my late teens, and my vision of an Anglican priesthood where women and men shared together in helping make God real to the people in the local community was put on hold. I settled on a career in the Probation Service, subsuming my frustrated ministerial calling in work with a particularly rejected and needy section of society. My love–hate relationship with the institutional Church flourished and faltered by turns; I was able to train for non-stipendiary ministry and was eventually made a deaconess, working in my home parish whilst continuing my employment in the Probation Service. In company with many others, I remained convinced that God was not playing games with the many women who were experiencing calls to ordained ministry, and I worked for the legislative changes that would allow those vocations to be received. My own journey in ministry took me into full-time work in Salisbury, as Cathedral Deacon and Director of a fast-growing innovative Christian Education Centre, and more recently to the Ely Diocese where I am joint Diocesan Director of Ordinands and Bishop's Director of

Women's Ministry, with a pastoral and liturgical base at Great
St Mary's, the University Church in Cambridge. Now, more
than thirty-five years on, the love–hate relationship is as
real, even though the dreams of the opening up of the priesthood for women in the Church of England have become a
reality.

As I write this, in the weeks approaching my priesting, I find
myself reflecting upon what it will be like when on Trinity
Sunday, for the first time, I will be able to preside at the Parish
Communion Service at Great St Mary's. I have a strong feel for
the history of the place. So much has happened over the centuries
in this building. It will not only be a first for me: it will be a
first for the congregation and a first for the building. It will be
in part a renewal of the place. I will be standing in a long line
of very eminent former vicars and curates, as for the first time
behind the altar a woman's voice will say those so familiar words:
'This is my body, which is given for you.' And in churches up
and down the country, in market towns, small villages and urban
over-spill areas, women's voices will be 'doing this in remembrance of Christ', and, by doing it afresh, they will be bringing
the whole of humanity into the completeness of the celebration
of the Eucharist. It will perhaps be a moment of apprehension, of
scarcely contained emotion; it will certainly be a moment of great
joy and personal fulfilment.

Women's voices

During the last few months I have been privileged to gain very
rich insights into the nature of priesthood and a variety of
understandings about what constitute priestly functions, from the
twenty-five women deacons in the Ely Diocese with whom I have
been engaged in an individual process of discerning their own
vocation to priesthood in advance of the forthcoming ordinations.
This has offered me a unique opportunity to hear the voices of
other women as they prepared for the priesthood, and much
of what I have to say in this paper is based upon what they have
told me, as well as upon my own experiences.

A number of the women are in pastoral charge of parishes or
specific communities. For them, much of the focus of priesthood

has centred on the Eucharist and the present dil
encounter in 'finding a male priest to say the m
Sunday after Sunday. 'It feels', said one 'like going
a begging bowl.' 'It's so frustrating', another voiced
hard all week at collaboration and inclusiveness in min. .y and
communication, and then on Sundays to have to stand there on
tenterhooks, wondering if it will all be over-turned.' Many women
expressed a sense of incompleteness in their present ministry.
They can pastor, they can preach, but they cannot preside; and
yet all these things should have a unity and a wholeness,
and should come together in the sacramental worship of the
gathered church. One woman spoke most movingly of reaching
out day by day to the brokenness of the community she serves,
but not being able on Sundays to offer that brokenness at the
altar, for it to be joined to the brokenness of Christ and healed
by his love and his life. Part of the circle was missing.

For other women, presiding at the Eucharist, whilst being seen
as an enormous privilege, was not felt to be the most momentous
part of the step they would be taking. For those who are developing a ministry of spiritual direction and personal counselling,
and who see an increasing role in the sacrament of reconciliation,
to be able with the full authority and backing of the Church to
pronounce an absolution after confession, is almost more important than being able to preside at communion. As far as the
missing chapter of the Church's ministry is concerned, the
'ABC'—Absolution, Blessing and Consecration—few made any
mention of now being able to bless people and congregations in
the 'you' rather than 'us' form. As one woman said, 'In our
church everyone is always "blessing" everyone else all the time
any way!'

For women deacons, many of whom have been in licensed
ministry for a good number of years, the step into priesthood is
scarcely a move into alien territory. The margin between what
has been and what is to come is a narrow one. One woman felt
that for ages she had been a priest-in-waiting. For many women
the long years of waiting have been frustrating; for some of
course it has all come too late, and that includes those who have
given up and left the Church, and others long since retired from
active ministry. For some women the years of waiting have been

opportunities for growth into a greater maturity and God-given time for preparing for what lies ahead. One woman felt that what she could now offer in priesthood was so much richer than it might have been a dozen or so years earlier.

And with the possibility of priesthood for women, the sense of injustice that has troubled many will be dealt with; and especially for those presently on the edges of the gathered church, priesthood will have been given a new legitimacy and credibility.

God calls: the Church orders

For me there are two aspects to an understanding of God's call to priesthood. First, I believe God calls people to minister, not specifically as deacons or as priests, or indeed as bishops, but simply to commit themselves to the task of helping make God real for people, to keep the God-connection as strong as possible—to keep the rumour of God alive—by serving the community in which they are living and working with compassion and in love. God calls us to ministry and the Church in its wisdom orders that ministry and determines what form it should most appropriately take, given the gifts, skills, experience and circumstances of the potential minister, in relation to the needs of the church community. Before 1987 the Church deemed it right that women called to ministry were accredited as lay ministers or made deaconesses; from the spring of 1987 the diaconal order of ministry was opened to women; and after 22 February 1994, women have legally been able to be ordained priests in the Church of England. God calls: the Church orders.

My long journey of ministry has taken me along a corridor, in which a number of locked doors have at times barred the way to proceeding further. Sometimes with others I have helped in pushing against some of the closed doors, and when it has been deemed right, or when there has been sufficient pressure applied in the right places, a door has swung open and I have gone through into a new stretch of ministerial corridor. Now the door to priesthood is open, and, if my journey is still to continue, it seems appropriate to pass through that door and discover the new adventure in ministry that awaits on the other side. So for me, and for many deacons with whom I have spoken, without in any sense minimizing the importance of this next step, it may be that one question to be asked about priesthood is 'Well, why not?' After all, the expectation for male deacons has always been that after a short period in the diaconate preparing themselves for presbyteral ministry, they would duly proceed to priesthood. The situation facing deacons of the female gender only looks more complicated because many have been in diaconal ministry for seven or more years, and because there are well over one thousand of us going through the door at much the same time.

If one aspect of priesthood is the calling out of priestly gifts by God and of the responding to that call, then a second aspect is the important underpinning by the Church of that call. Again and again deacons shared with me a sense of already being received as a priest by their local community: 'You *are* our lady vicar.' For the majority, the ministerial gifts they are already exercising, and have been developing over the years, are essentially *priestly* gifts; gifts in leadership, in preaching and teaching, in offering wise counsel and spiritual advice, in acting as a focus for reconciliation, in being alongside people at points of crisis and transition in their lives, in administration. These gifts, offered to the community, are used and valued and affirmed. And in some situations the community has recognized the woman as the priest for them, as *their* priest, almost before she has got there herself. The community then endorses God's call to priesthood, and the Church through its agreed processes of testing and discerning of priestly vocations finally fulfils that call through the episcopal imposition of hands and the grace of orders in ordination.

A total offering

So what will it have felt like, beneath the octagon of Ely Cathedral, when my Diocesan bishop ordains me priest, and I am surrounded by my fellow women deacons, and I hope a goodly gathering of family and friends adding to the great crowd who will almost certainly be there? It will be a time of great joy and celebration. Perhaps I will be taken back in thought to that point when as a young teenager preparing for confirmation, I caught a glimpse of what it might be that God was calling *me* to, as I watched the priest presiding at the altar. At that time, in the mid-1950s, I was soon disabused of the possibility of women having a priestly vocation. However, in training for social work and in my early years as a Probation Officer, I came to see that God was to be discovered in the messiest of situations and people—and that the Church by no means had the prerogative when it came to caring with compassion and love for people in trouble, and to addressing the need for economic and structural changes to bring about a greater sense of justice and equality in society. I came to see that my work as a Probation Officer, if offered to God, *was* indeed ministry.

What I hope for now is that at my priesting I will be able to take into that service of ordination *all* my experiences, secular and church: my strengths and skills, my vulnerability and short-comings, and the whole of my personhood—my gender and sexuality. In moving into this new stage of ministry I want to feel that with God there will no longer be anything left on hold, that I am offering all that has been, all that is, and all that is still to come to God's continuing service; and that with the grace and blessing of priestly orders I will be able to continue to grow to be the woman that God would have serve him as a priest in his Church. In the words of the Alternative Service Book Ordinal, it was indeed 'long ago that I began to weigh and ponder all this'. I am 'fully determined by the grace of God, to give myself wholly to his service and devote to him my best powers of mind and spirit . . . so that with the assistance of his Holy Spirit, I may grow up into his likeness'.

When I look back on my years in ministry—and I include those valuable years in the Probation Service equally with my work more clearly identified as overt Church-based ministry—I am less aware of having planned the route for myself, and more sensing that the way has been chosen and guided by God. After all, I would feel much less comfortable in my present posts if I had not had those years of practice, teaching, administration and student selection and training in the Probation Service. In the divine economy none of the past has been lost; it is all being used in renewing the place, and it will all be taken into this new chapter of priesthood.

The shadow of the spire

After four or five years of busy and fulfilling ministry as a non-stipendiary deaconess, it was something of a surprise to find myself invited to be on the staff of Salisbury Cathedral and to exchange the back streets of Harrow and Wembley for the beauties of a Cathedral Close.

If it was a surprise for me, then I suppose it was quite a shock to the system for others, when seven hundred and fifty years of tradition at Salisbury Cathedral were challenged by the appearance of an ordained woman on the staff. There were the inevitable difficulties about evolving an appropriate liturgical role: where I should sit during particular services; how I should be styled; what I could wear (could I 'cope' or not?). The problems of 'going invisible'—finding myself omitted from the rubrics of a service, for instance—were reasonably easily dealt with. Gradually the congregation and clergy got used to my presence, and even on occasions indicated they valued it. I well remember an early encounter with an elderly retired canon. He muttered under his breath in an audible aside, 'In my day, deacons knew their place!' The response which I should like to have made, but which only formulated itself a gin and tonic later, was 'Well, in my day, deacons are having to re-new their place'.

I had a very rich and fulfilling six years at Salisbury, but looking back I can see that my ministry was more readily accepted when I behaved like an honorary male: when I did not push my male colleagues too hard to address feelings, when I allowed the cerebral and intellectual to dominate the emotional and intuitive. As with many men, they operated a 'problem-solving' approach to most of our corporate life. On the occasion of the Archbishop of Canterbury coming to Salisbury to consecrate a new suffragan bishop, a legal official who had taken part in the ceremony refused at the distribution of communion to take the chalice from me. Dr Runcie had given him the bread, I presented the chalice, and he shook his head at me in disapproval. That did happen from time to time, but I had not anticipated it on that occasion, and I discovered I was not as immune to feelings of rejection as I would have liked. At a subsequent staff meeting when I shared this with my colleagues, I received an interesting range of responses. One suggested I might be just a bit paranoid: perhaps *I* was the problem, rather than the other's refusal to accept the chalice. Another offered to go and 'duff up' the offending communicant; he was presumably feeling the challenge of 'our woman' having been maltreated in this way. A third proceeded patiently to tell me why some people felt like this, in no way acknowledging that I just might already have done some thinking of my own about this sort of happening, nor that I might have *feelings* about what had transpired. In fact I had already had a previous conversation about the chalice refusal, at lunch after the consecration service. Dr George Carey, then a newish bishop, asked how I coped when such things occurred; it had never happened to him, and he seemed genuinely concerned to be able to identify with the experiences of women ministers. He wanted to know how I *felt* when someone chose not to receive the consecrated wine from me. It felt very good and supportive to be able to share with him.

One of my sadnesses about that chapter of ministry in Salisbury is that I did not ever really discover or feel able to work at what it was to be a *woman* clergyperson in a cathedral, although I am in no doubt at all of the importance of ordained women serving in cathedrals, nor of the value of what I was personally able to offer in my time in Salisbury.

Challenging fears and taboos

In the future there will continue to be conflicts in facing the sexuality inherent in relationships between women priests and others. For some men, women are seen primarily as sex objects, or unapproachable icons: paradigms of Eve or Mary. Women priests will challenge deeply held unconscious fears and taboos, primal echoes of 'magic' women. Men who are threatened by strong, competent women (the honorary 'male' woman priest), and may prefer the more dependent 'little woman at home', whom they can protect and feel manly with, are likely to be equally challenged by the 'dolly-bird' priest, with high heels and dangly earrings chosen with care to match her chasuble. Will women priests be able to keep their gender integrity, whilst occupying what some would wish to be a non-sexual role? The conflicts will need of course to be faced not only by the men of the congregation; they will be equally challenging for other women.

And which aspects of the primary power of the *mother* role will be taken into priesthood by women? Fears of castration, of dominance and dependence, will fight alongside wishes for nurturing, enabling, being allowed to grow in safety and security and to achieve independence, and to move into mature adult-to-adult relationships. Where will the menstrual cycle fit in here, with its often pervasive influence on a woman's capacity for effective working? I think I will need to discover how to listen to my body better, so that I take into priesthood my own rhythmic cycle of judging when for me are the most creative times of the month, and when it might be best to make major decisions.

What, I wonder, will it be like to see a woman actually presiding at the altar, no longer in an assistant or peripheral position? It will be significantly different from seeing the deacon there, despite her well-developed pastoral and preaching role. For some it will signify that now the *whole* of humanity is involved in the offering by the whole community of the whole of its life: its pain and brokenness, its joy and celebration. For others, the symbol and meaning and message of the woman behind the altar will challenge a deeply held belief in their understanding of the essential maleness of God.

The gifts we bring

I hope to be able to take into priesthood experiences of the minister as servant as well as shepherd, and to bring with me all that I have learned in a long diaconate. It has taken me quite a journey to discover that it really is legitimate to trust one's feelings, and that intuition is to be prized. If I am able to continue working at achieving a balance between the cerebral and the emotional in my approach to life, that I believe will be a gift that I bring to priesthood.

Part of my vision for a priesthood which includes women alongside men, is the valuing of *being* as much as *doing*. The present role models for priesthood seem to encourage *activity* as a mark of evaluating success in ministry. Doubtless there will be workaholic women priests keeping company with their male counterparts. Whilst in no sense denying the capacity of many good male priests to give high priority to things of the inner life, my hope is that with the coming of women priests, God-centred things of the Spirit may have a greater emphasis; that time for prayer, for meditation and for teaching others things that may deepen their connection to God will have more space and a higher profile. My experience suggests that women may bring particular gifts in the area of spiritual direction and retreat-leading—aspects of faith for which many church people and others are showing themselves to have a great hunger.

Connected to this are the gifts women will bring in offering creative liturgies, new forms and approaches to worship, which are inclusive in language, participative in design, and alive in their imagery and understanding of God.

Another gift which is, I believe, more often found in women than in men is the wish to make connections and to work holistically. In conversations there is a greater tendency for men to compete with and cap each other's stories, whilst women in the main add to and complement what is being said, including and gathering in members of the circle. Women have therefore, in my view, a particular contribution to make in good adult education in the Church, developing group work and opportunities for faith exploration and theological reflection which start where people are and encourage maximum participation and the sharing of leadership and responsibility in learning.

A vision for the future

I have a vision for the Church's ministry, enriched and extended by women priests, which develops along lines that are non-competitive, non-hierarchical and non-paternalistic. My present experience is that many inter-clergy relationships are threatened by a sense of the other being felt to be more 'successful' in his ministry. It *is* difficult to know whether the hours spent in pastoral encounters, in preparing sermons, in writing letters for the parish magazine, are being as profitably used as possible. In the Church we are only slowly developing tools adequate for self-appraisal, and for evaluating the tasks of ministry; it is only too easy to fall back on comparing numbers of those presented for confirmation, and to counting 'bums on pews' and hoping they are as many as attended worship last Sunday, last Christmas, a year ago. . .

It may well be the case that over recent years the institutional Church has become less concerned with status and hierarchy: that is certainly a trend I hope will be encouraged by the inclusion of women in the Anglican priesthood here. In many congregations the 'Father-knows-best' model of parish organization and clergy— lay relationships still continues. My hope is for a much greater equality and power-sharing to develop among the gathered Christians who make up the local church; for the fostering of 'adult-to-adult' relationships, rather than dependent 'parent-to-child' ones; for Christians to be firstly recognized as *persons* rather than as gender-centred women or men.

Moving into stipendiary ministry after a varied career in the Probation Service which spanned more than twenty years, was quite a shock to the system. For a good many years—before it was fashionable, and indeed before it was a legal requirement— the Probation Service was an 'equal opportunities employer', in every sense of that phrase: both in relation to employment opportunities and the development of one's career, and also in how one's particular skills could be best used in working with clients. As a relatively new Senior Probation Officer, I had the chance of helping develop an innovative and creative management structure which allowed a team of Probation Officers to discover a genuinely collaborative style of working together. Starting with the assumption that people worked best when they were in the main doing things they enjoyed doing, wanted to do, and which maximized the use of their particular gifts, skills and experiences, we began by together listing all the tasks that were required of these sixteen Probation Officers in this particular probation 'patch'. We then helped the officers individually, and working with trusted others from the team, to list and recognize and own their personal skills and interests which could be contributed to carrying out the overall tasks of the office. What we eventually discovered, after some hours spent in discussion on 'away days', was that the sum total of the skills offered matched almost exactly the office workload. We then, over time, developed a system

which moved from all Probation Officers doing an almost identical job of work, irrespective of particular gifts and interests, to
a differentiated sharing out of office tasks to maximize individual
potential and experience. This seemed to lead to much less
internal 'rivalry' and much greater mutual support developing
between colleagues; to a sense of greater purposefulness about
the office; and to a growth in self-confidence, and a giving of
affirmation amongst officers who now felt themselves to be, and
were accorded as being, experts in specific aspects of the work
of the Probation Service. Perhaps most significant, there was a
general growing sense of contentment in working relationships,
and stress levels and consequently time taken off on sick leave
dropped quite perceptibly.

My vision for an enriched church ministry is that we develop
models of working, like that in the Probation Service, which are
truly collaborative, and which are reflected in parish structures,
in liturgy, in language, in the shape of pastoral care, in styles of
outreach; models which are essentially open, affirming, trusting
and nurturing, and where responsibility is really shared.

Potential pitfalls

Of course ordaining women to priesthood in itself may do little
to change the outlook and practice of the clergy. One of my
nightmares is that so seductively powerful is the institution of
the Church, that women may simply be sucked into male patterns
of clericalism, and be unable (rather than unwilling) to resist
being coloured by the dominant culture espoused by many of
our clerical brothers. Those who for years have been excluded
from sharing in the power can sometimes abuse it or collude
with it when it becomes theirs. It may be that for some women,
having waited for so long and become exhausted in the process,
a degree of complacency will take over: 'We've got there at last!'
My hope is that we will never lose our capacity to identify with
the powerless, and will learn how to take real responsibility in
exercising such power as I believe is given in priesthood. This
suggests moving away from a possessive understanding of 'my'
people and 'my' church; to holding on to the vision of a Church
which really is founded on a belief in the value and equality of

all; to being prepared in all humility to learn from others, to trust others' gifts and their capacity for development, and genuinely to share with others and delegate to them; and to working at developing models of ministry where power and influence are as widely disseminated and shared as possible.

It will all take a long while. The vision of a renewed Church will only be briefly glimpsed with the first ordinations of women to priesthood in the Church of England, and will only slowly grow over succeeding generations. In the Lutheran Church in Germany where there have been ordained women for many years now, there is still prejudice against women which makes it difficult for them to be appointed to senior positions; and similar stories are told in other parts of the world-wide Anglican communion. Traditions which for centuries have held women as being inferior and needing to be carefully controlled and subordinated, coupled with a hierarchical structure of ministry, suggest that for some years to come women may find themselves junior partners to their male colleagues. My developing vision of the ministry of the Church includes a hope that it is soon opened to allow for the possibility of women bishops. It seems quite illogical now to have women excluded from this last remaining order of ministry; to retain a male-only episcopate perpetuates a divisive approach to the integrity of our ancient understanding of a three-fold order of ministry.

My vision of a renewed Church of the future, where women are seen to be sharing in the guidance and leadership of the Church at all levels, and in a variety of situations, does not omit an awareness of the inevitable difficulties that will continue to face the thousand-plus new pioneering women priests. Many will experience subtle and not so subtle forms of prejudice, rejection and hostility; that has been the lot of women in the Church for a good many years now, and women have learned and grown through those experiences and used them to good effect in their ministry.

As women priests help to rediscover the place of priesthood, and of how that relates to the ministry of *all* baptized Christian believers, so we need to be alert to the dangers of becoming male clones, of being unwittingly drawn into old, traditional, paternalistic and hierarchical models of priesthood. To begin with, there will be few female role models to guide us: as with our ordination to the diaconate, when the path ahead was scarcely charted, and the journey to be made across unknown territory, so with our priesting, there will be enormous support from others to help us along, and primarily of course from members of our congregations and fellow clergy. It is worth regularly reminding ourselves that at least 70 per cent of church members are positively in favour of the ordination of women to priesthood, and a probably considerably higher percentage than that in most congregations that have an ordained women member of staff. The greater proportion of regular church members want women priests and will be doing all they can to encourage our ministry and to aid the process of our reception into the wider Church. That will be important to remember if we occasionally find ourselves in difficult situations with those who remain unhappy about women priests, or who wish to continue denying the validity of our priestly orders. That will be particularly true for women who find themselves working in isolation from other women priests. Certainly to begin with, ordained women, who comprise about a tenth of the total number of Anglican clergy in England, will rarely be working alongside other women. Those who work in teams and group ministries will usually have as colleagues men only. Experience indicates that even the most supportive and sensitive of male colleagues can only partially identify with some of the particular difficulties that can be faced by women ministers. That suggests the need for careful thought to be given to where newly ordained women priests will get the necessary supports for their ministry. Even assuming that future developments continue to move away from the individualistic working of one vicar in one parish, and lead to more clergy working collaboratively in teams, where the tasks of parish ministry are shared with fellow clergy and lay people, women priests will, I believe, still need their own support systems beyond the immediate local team. And that will be even more crucial for those women who find themselves working on their own, for instance in small rural parishes or deprived urban areas.

I am not wishing to advocate an unnecessary separation out of women clergy from our male colleagues—indeed much support will hopefully come from a variety of sources, which will include clergy and lay, male as well as female; but I do see the need, at least in the short term, for peer-group identification and support—for small cells, for diocesan-based gatherings, for a national network for women priests, possibly developing phoenix-like from the ashes of the former Movement for the Ordination of Women. Women priests will need safe places to explore our growing understanding of priesthood, an occasional shoulder to cry on, people with whom we can pray and yell, be angry, express our frustrations, share the pain and hurts and the fun and joy of it all. There will be so much to learn from one another and to offer back to the Church. With the right supports, some of the difficulties might be put into appropriate perspective, and the cutting edge of our ministerial gifts kept sharply honed.

Time for renewal

It is bound to take time for women to move into greater leadership roles in the Church with real authority. It will take time for the proportion of women to men in ordained ministry to increase to the point where a better balance is achieved, and women are less of a minority. This new step into priesthood is another staging post in the long journey that women have over the years been taking into ministry, and the journey continues. With it comes the possibility of an enriched and enlarged understanding of the nature of God; a greater completeness and credibility in our understanding of priesthood; opportunities to work at the complementarity of the genders in gifts given and received in ministry; a legitimization of the presbyteral gifts that women have been developing over the years.

As women grow in confidence in their exercise of old skills and their discovery of new ones, and as they bring to the priesthood of the Church new insights into working together, my dearest hope is that not only for women, but for men also, clergy and lay, a liberation will be experienced which brings the Kingdom just a little nearer. It takes men and women together to create new life: with women and men together in priesthood, there can be a vision of a Church, newly created, re-created, bubbling with energy and creativity. My love–hate relationship with the Church continues. I take that into priesthood, and with it the potential to share in bringing the vision into being, in encouraging the new life that is the promise of God's Kingdom: in helping to renew the place.

6

Lady into fox: friends into priests

JANE WILLIAMS

Ten years ago I went to America, eager to experience the priestly ministry of women. I went hoping I might find it ordinary and natural, fearing I might find it strange and uncomfortable. But whatever else happened, I was sure that I would feel *represented* in a new way by a member of my own sex at the altar. What I had not expected was that it would emphasize my exclusion from the mysterious clerical caste. Yet that is exactly what it did.

The woman priest celebrated the coming of God among us using words that I can never say, and I knelt before her and received his body into my hands. Of course I did. And after the service, in beautifully-cut black with a large white clerical collar, she took my priest husband on one side to ask his advice and compare notes with him on a whole range of professional matters. Of course she did.

And I felt a pathetic desire to shout, like a small child, 'Pay attention *to me*', as though, because we were both women I had expected that bond to be greater than the clerical one. I also felt an equally pathetic desire to produce my degree certificate, proving that I, too, could talk theology, even without a collar.

It was a sobering experience, not least because it was so unexpected. It revealed not only the depths of my lack of self-knowledge, but also how little thought I had actually given to what I expected from women priests. Clearly, without articulating it, I had expected to feel an 'insider', brought into the heart of the Church by the presence there of another woman. But was this in any way a proper expectation? Or will it form the basis of yet another guilt-trip to lay on those women who are now taking up their priestly ministry in the Church of England, as though they did not have enough laid at their door already?

Inevitably and rightly women priests will join a professional club when they are priested. They will, generally, wear the clothes, do the tasks, join the meetings, wield the authority, that male priests have. And equally inevitably, they will need to discuss these things with those who share them. So perhaps my reaction is just an unresolved childishness, a desire for the Church to be 'mother' now, although I have so constantly and vociferously said that I am a grown-up, and do not need it to be 'father'?

Part of the problem, of course, is the length of time that the whole business has taken in England. For pretty well the whole of my adult life I have worked and written and spoken about how the Church needs women priests. And much of that has been in the company of women waiting to have their vocations officially tested. I have seen how the local community to which they minister has called them, and how the wider Church has need of their particular skills, and the living theology and the theology on the page have come together into an increasingly convincing whole. I am glad for the Church and I am glad for my friends, but I shall miss those years of cameraderie, and everything they taught us.

For example, they taught us that sometimes those of us who had no vocation to the priesthood could actually stand up and be bold on behalf of our sisters. Nobody could accuse us of overweening ambition, or threaten us with a perpetual curacy in an empty church three miles outside the exclusion zone for women priests round Walsingham. Organizations like the Movement for the Ordination of Women were remarkable for the degree to which they nurtured shared leadership, shared responsibility. There was no premature separating of those who would 'go on' to priesthood when the time came, and those of us who would 'stay behind'. Tasks were allotted on the basis of skills, opportunities, willingness and other such revolutionary principles so seldom applied in the wider councils of the Church. Working together like this has been an important experience of sisterhood for many of us, an experience of community, and so an experience, importantly, of 'church' for many for whom 'The Church' was unable and unwilling to provide such lived examples of sharing.

But now the time has come, the time for which so many of us have worked so long, the time for women to be priests, and to serve the Church in a different way from those of us who are called to be laypeople. And so, I think, the time has also come to remind ourselves of the basics. Why is it important that women should be priests? What do we expect of our priestly sisters? How far should they be burdened with the flag of our expectations, and when should they challenge us to remember their special calling?

I have supported the movements to ordain women for a number of reasons. First, because the arguments against the ordination of women seem to me to have grown increasingly heretical, to the point where they deny the central, shocking, saving fact of Christianity—that *God* became *human*. Instead, we are so often told that he became *a man*—a very different thing, apparently, from an ordinary human being, and requiring far less self-emptying love than the common old idea of incarnation. 'And can it be that I should gain / an interest in my saviour's blood? / Died he for me, who caused such pain, / for me who him to death betrayed?' Well, no, it cannot be. Not unless you are male, apparently. Now, clearly, this will not do.

So, second, I have supported the ordination because throughout Christian history, God has called women to be full members of the Church, made fully responsible, with all fellow Christians, for preaching the good news. Quite often I have felt in myself and seen in other women the desire to retreat into 'femininity', as though by being good 'women'—daughters, wives, mothers, defined by our relationship with men—we are fulfilling our purpose as created beings. The Gospel tells us we are not. We are all called to define ourselves primarily in relation to God, and to God's community. Feminine laziness and patronizing masculinity must not collude to allow women off the hook of discipleship.

But next, and perhaps most persistently, I have supported the ordination of women because of the women-in-waiting themselves. I have seen my friends, with their great commitment, sustained against such odds, to the Church that has nourished them. They have grown to great maturity on that food, however grudgingly it was sometimes given. When I have looked, with terrible indecision, at the good and faithful laypeople and priests whom the Church will lose, or who will feel dreadfully compromised when priesthood is shared with women, I have been brought back, again and again, to see the women priests waiting. They have a great variety of gifts—some of gentleness, some of tenderness, some of sensitivity, some of intellect, some of acuity, some of power. They have years and years of experience. I wish the Church did not have to choose, since it quite obviously needs all the help it can get; but I do not honestly see how it could do without the priestly gifts of half the human race for ever.

Lastly, I have supported the ordination of women because the Church is supposed to show forth God's love and God's judgement to the world. In the modern western world, not to ordain women is to indicate that God is on the side of those forces that undervalue women, that rate their gifts as secondary, expendable, that assume they have no real interests of their own, and can be subordinated to the interests of those who matter—the powerful, the men. In that sense, I see the ordination of women as a matter of sacramental symbolism: an 'outward and visible sign of an inward and spiritual grace'. Women priests are, for many, the outward sign of God's love, and a particularly appropriate sign in a world that is increasingly tempted to renege on its 'communist' commitments to justice and equality for all, now that the going has got tough. In the wider arena, there are noticeable signs of a fundamentalist backlash in all parties, religious and political, and the rights of all marginal groups, including women, inevitably suffer.[1] Similarly, in this country, as recession bites and fear grows, it is the people on the edge who are targeted and blamed— the blacks, the gays, the women. For the Church of England to decide to ordain women at just this moment is, for once, a piece of inspired timing, a signal of just what God's love must mean, at all times and in all places. It is the kind of love that searches for one lost coin, one lost sheep, that forgives a dying penitent thief, that says 'the poor shall inherit the earth', that gives its whole future into the hands of stupid people, even to the point of death. Women priests, in a world that still cannot value women, or anyone else without economic power, become a particularly potent symbol of that love of God.

It is this symbolic job that will change, quite quickly, I suspect, after women have been ordained. The women who have been waiting to be priested have had nothing in common except their exclusion. Of course, they were all women, but that did not mean that they had any experiences in common, apart from the experience of having their vocation belittled. Some of them are old, some young; some are rich, some poor; some are academics, some not; some are mothers, some not. There is no one experience of 'being a woman' that you can point to and say 'This is what women will bring to the Church'. What they will bring, and what the Church desperately needs, is *themselves*—all their range of gifts, their range of experiences, their own individual humanity. Just the same things that male priests bring, in fact.

But the first generation or so of women priests will also, of course, bring their symbolic value as outsiders who have been brought in, of dispossessed children who have been taken back into the bosom of the family. When, as priests, they break the bread that must be broken so that the body can be gathered together again from the ends of the earth, they will be particularly powerful signs of God's seeking love. Like the first non-Jewish Christian priests, like the first slave-priests, so the first women priests will be signs that God's love for us is constantly so much bigger than our love for each other. They will challenge the barriers we put up to try to prevent God from being God.

But soon, very soon, they will be 'the Church' again. For so long, women have been the prophets, hammering at the gates, shouting out God's message; but now they will be the priests who sweep out the inner courts of God's sanctuary. Will it be their job to keep those gates shut against the next wave of hammerers and shouters? Part of the function of the priesthood is to guard, preserve and hand down what has been entrusted to them by previous generations. They are, through their ordination vows, made 'conservatives'. Now this is not necessarily an insult. Good things from the past must be conserved. But it will be a dramatic change of role. For so long would-be women priests have been called radicals, have been accused of pulling down the edifice of the past. Most of them have not seen it that way, of course. They have seen themselves as bringing to growth seeds planted throughout the Christian past. But now that the plant has come to fruition, their task is presumably one of conservation again.

Honesty compels us to admit that women will no longer symbolize God's love for the oppressed once they have been priested. They will, of course, still preach of it. And, of course, women will still be oppressed, in this country and all over the world. But women who are *inside*, even if only by the skin of their teeth, cannot and should not expect to hold out the innocent, supplicatory hands of those outside. This is nothing to lament. No one group should have to carry the symbolic weight of being God's suffering servants for ever. But the temptation is to hold onto that moral stature long after our role has clearly shifted.

When there are women priests, women must admit *responsibility* for the Church in a new way. We have been in the enviable position of powerlessness. We have been able to enjoy the Church's benefits while disclaiming complicity in its idiocies. No longer. We will now be as guilty as the rest of them. This applies in very obvious ways to women clergy, but I think there is a significant change for laywomen, too. We will no longer be able to lay the blame at 'their' door, in a simplistic kind of way.[2] If our sisters are involved in the processes that not only represent God to the world, but also misrepresent him, then we can no longer blame 'the men', and assure ourselves that we could do it better. Instead, we have to admit that the imperfections of the Church are part of its very nature, and that we are as much responsible for it as anyone.

This is, I am convinced, a positive step. It is one more way in which women can grow up. Part of the pain of being adult is to be held responsible for your commitments. For a great many years now, women have been committed to the Church but not responsible for it, and we must now change. So how will we handle our new adulthood? Will we use it to do to others what has been done to us? Those who have opposed the ordination of women have often spoken sneeringly of 'the pain' of women waiting to be priested. That pain is by no means over, in a Church that is trying to accommodate two irreconcilable views. But I was shocked to see exactly the same rhetoric being used by 'our' side about those opposed to women priests. Their 'pain' was derided, and their right to stay in the Church challenged, just as ours has been all these years.

And the reason why I found this so shocking, apart from its innate uncharitableness, is that it called into question the value of all those years in the wilderness. Have we learnt nothing of what it is to be outsiders, to be rejected and unvalued? Is there no way of admitting that, while the Church has certainly made the right decision—to ordain women—still it is a place of reconciliation, and that women, above all, have learned the value of reconciliation? Now that we have 'won', is binding up the wounded no longer very high on our list? I realize the 'victory' is illusory for many women deacons, and that many women are actually suffering more hatred and abuse since the Synod vote than ever before, but it still worries me how the machinery for rejecting and despising our opponents is being put in place, ready for use in battle.

This is bound up with what was said earlier about symbolism. If women will no longer symbolize the presence of God among the outcast, then they can at least be sensitive to look for God among such people. If they cannot, then their own years of struggle have been wasted, theologically speaking. They will not have taken with them into the priesthood of the Church that central fact, the one that we can never get through to our hearts and our minds, and that is that God became *human*. And that means human not just as I am, whether I am male or female, lay or priest, black or white, liberal or conservative, but also human as 'they' are, 'they' my opposite, 'they' whom I consider wrong.

This could easily be read, of course, as the woolliest, most contentless kind of theology. It sounds as though I am saying that we must tolerate all opinions, however apparently contrary to all we hold true. But that is not my intention. I believe that much of the opposition to women priests has been theologically inept. It rests on a desire to make God abide by the rules that we have formulated, while the whole history of God's dealing with the human race, as shown us in the Old and New Testaments, is clear that God's own rules are so unfathomable as to look anarchic. The priesting of women has been an important

enlargement of our theological imaginations. But the process
cannot and will not stop there. What the next challenge to our
attempts to enclose God will be we cannot yet see. But I would
love to think that women will be at the forefront of that endeavour, too, because of what they have learned in this struggle. I
hope they will not become the new grumblers, the ones who
have got God where they want him and are not going to allow
him to change any more.

For my money, the next arena will be the ecumenical one. The
one really serious point that opponents of the ordination of
women have had is that two of the great Christian Churches, the
Roman Catholic and the Orthodox, are opposed to it. We believe
that what the Anglican Church and other Churches that ordain
women have done is symbolic for the whole Church. It is symbolic not only because to deny the priesthood to women is to
deny the fullness of God's incarnation, but also because the
Church has become all too adept at fudging hard truths in
the interests of compromise. Some things are too important to
be compromised, and the ordination of women was one of them.

But the call to let the truth blaze out is not the Church's only
vocation. What of the need to show God's unity to the world?
Those of us who have fought for the ordination of women must
now fight with equal vigour for the uniting of God's Church, or
else our struggle will look suspiciously like self-seeking.

So let me return to the question with which I started. What
do we hope for from women priests, and which of our expectations must be exposed as childish and impossible?

At the heart of this question lies another, I suspect. Will these,
our sisters, still be women first or will they now be priests first?
But, of course, that is a false question. If by 'women' we mean
people who are only identified by their sex, irrespective of their
differences, their talents, their experiences, then I hope the term
'women priests' will be replaced by the single word 'priests'. I
hope the Church will now be able to see each individual who
offers herself for what she is, not what she represents. But equally,
if the word 'priest' means someone who holds status and power
in relation to the rest of us, the laity, then I hope women priests
will think seriously about the history of shared ministry that lies
behind the great campaign to bring women into the priesthood.

Priests and laypeople are called to serve God in different ways, but they need each other, and it is only together that they make the Church.

For very many women, Christian and non-Christian alike, women priests will continue to symbolize some kind of acceptance of their own sexuality. For some, this acceptance will be a sign of God's own acceptance. For others, who are less interested in 'God', it will still be a sign, a sign of a shift in attitudes to women in our western culture that has been so dominated by one-sided and derogatory images of our sex. Christianity has helped to form and been formed by that culture, so that change at the heart of its symbol-system has repercussions far beyond the Church's own boundaries. Either way, it is a symbol change of huge imaginative importance. But it can only continue to work like that insofar as these new priests make the symbolic acceptance concrete in their own ministry. Just as it was possible for a woman Prime Minister to preside over a decade that actually made life harder for most other women in the country, so it will be perfectly possible for women priests to minister in a Church that continues to give little value to women, or, indeed, to lay people of either sex. Women priests cannot any longer be abstract symbols. They have to be made to *work*.

Perhaps this is asking rather a lot of women priests. But then again, perhaps not. They have taken on the public task of representing God to the Church and to the world, but they have done so on behalf of all of us, just as all priests do. Their task is not different in kind from the task of all Christians; it is only different in the public, visible and unavoidable form it takes. If we laypeople are calling upon them to represent to us God's active love, acceptance and commitment to justice, then it is their priestly calling to turn to us and demand our support and energies for the same task. If we really want them to help to break down the barriers that keep us from properly valuing each other, then we must not complain if they demand time, trouble, money and effort from us in return. If we do not want a maternalistic Church in exchange for a paternalistic one, then we must not wriggle when our priests, male or female, ask us to grow up.

When I receive the priestly ministry of women friends in England,[3] I still hope that I may find it ordinary and natural, and I still fear that I may find it strange and uncomfortable. But above all, I still expect to feel myself 'represented' at the altar, not *just* because the priest will be a woman, but more importantly because she will be someone who demands of me the same commitment to our shared vision of God. And she will know that we, her lay sisters, are capable of meeting that demand, because we have struggled together to make part of that vision clear, in all the years of working together to bring women into the priesthood. And we will know she has the right to make such a demand of us because she is a priest in the Church of God, called to remind God's people constantly of the task to which we are committed. The task itself is the same as it has always been, to help the 'blind to see, the lame to walk and the poor to have the good news preached to them'.[4]

Notes

1 I owe this point, and doubtless much else in this paper, to Susan Dowell. Many of the issues raised here were aired during discussions for our book, *Bread, Wine and Women* (Virago, 1994).

2 Cf. Penny Nairne's article in the MOW magazine *Chrysalis* (July 1993), 'when our vicar is a woman, if she issues irritating orders, I won't be able to shrug them off with the thought that it's so like a man' (p. 10).

3 The Church in Wales, which I now belong to, has now made its decision to continue not to ordain women as priests.

4 Paraphrasing Matthew 11.4–6.

7
The seven devils of women's ordination
or
'She who lie down with dogs catch fleas'

MAGGIE ROSS

> Where the vision fails the people perish, but blessed are
> they who keep the law.
>
> (Prov 29.18)

The Church of England as an institution is dying. It has been
dying for a long time. It is dying because it has lost its vision.
It is dying because it neither wishes to acknowledge nor to do
anything about the seven devils that possess it. And because it
is self-absorbed, because it refuses to see itself clearly in the light
of the vision of God, it no longer serves as a moral force among
the people.[1] And the people perish.

Anglican morbidity, which reflects that of other British Christian institutions, affects every aspect of its life, including its
scholarship. For example, in what appears to be an act of unconscious eisegesis,[2] the translators of the New English Bible confused authority and power, spirit and law by interpreting this
verse, 'Where there is no one in authority, the people break
loose, but a guardian of the law keeps them on the straight path.'
The REB is slightly improved, but not much: 'With no one in
authority, the people throw off all restraint, but he who keeps
God's law leads them on a straight path.' The New Jerusalem
Bible: 'Where there is no vision the people get out of hand;
happy are they who keep the law.' The NRSV: 'Where there is
no prophecy, the people cast off restraint, but happy are those
who keep the law.' The Interlinear Hebrew Bible translates the

word for 'vision' as 'revelation', and perhaps this is closer to
the issue at hand: the revelation of the self-outpouring, humble
God in Christ.

On the other hand, the NEB translators may have had in mind
a passage in Hosea 4.6 that reflects both interpretations: 'Want
of knowledge [of God] has been the ruin of my people. As you
have rejected knowledge, so will I reject you as a priest to me.
As you have forsaken the teaching of God, so will I, your God,
forsake your children.'

From the dismal perspective of the end of 1993, this verse
could be interpreted, 'When clergy and those who ape them
listen only to themselves and refuse to acknowledge the vision
of God, transcendent and incarnate, as that from which everything else must be discerned and proceed, they implode into
their individual and collective ego-decoration, which substitutes
for worship, and, refusing to go beyond all images and concepts,
which characterizes true faith in the self-emptying God, they
worship the idols of their own self-image, trying to force other
people to follow suit by degrading them.'[3]

This interpretation is supported by Hos 4.7: 'The more priests
there are, the more they sin against me; their dignity I shall turn
into dishonour. They feed on the sin of my people and are
greedy for their iniquity. Priest and people will fare alike.' The
rest of the chapter is well worth reading.[4]

It might be argued that the last half of Proverbs 29.18 reads,
'blessed are they who keep the law', but as every student of the
Old Testament knows, it is the law written on the heart that
the words refer to, not the dualistic prescripts and strictures of
behavioural codes. It is precisely this point that Jesus makes in
his teaching and in his life. Each individual, no matter what their
status, is responsible for their own relationship with God, both
for themselves and for the sake of the community. Each is thus
responsible for leadership. In the church this used to be called
the *sensus fidei*, the responsibility of each person to open their
heart to receive their fragment of the revelation to share with
others, which common vision, more than anything else, was the
source of unity.

Perhaps even more pertinent, Jesus' ministry exposes the bank-
ruptcy of a hierarchical 'priesthood', which, in the name of God,

pointed to itself rather than God, and sought to control people by feeding on their fear of death, mediating forgiveness for a price. Jesus sets people free from the terror and imprisonment of the rule of law, and restores to them the vision by means of the Spirit, paying the price, and setting the example, with his own body and blood.

It is only because Jesus is a layman, and not of priestly or levitical inheritance, that he, by his obedience, can become the great high priest. And it is ironic and significant that the church founded in his name so quickly reverted to the old model. Those bent on control usually achieve power, and it is their writings which survive to be cited by subsequent generations bent on similar self-perpetuation, in other words, those least resembling the humble divinity they claim to represent.

And what of the liberation that is sacramentalized in the Eucharist? The sign of Christ's self-emptying, of his utter obedience in conforming his will to the will of his self-emptying Father?[5] His faithfulness to the vision beyond all worldly reason is again removed to the temple precincts, and again used to enslave the people. It should be noted that Christ's obedience is given freely, not in response to coercion. It is elicited, it is called forth, a response to the self-emptying of the Father, deep calling to deep, *kenosis* calling to *kenosis*. This is the *only* legitimate model for obedience; obedience has nothing to do with the oppression that has misused the name of obedience to perpetuate religious tyranny, slavery and degradation, whether physical, psychological or spiritual. Obedience (from the Latin 'to listen') has nothing to do with the attitude, 'Everyone in their slot, and all's right with the world.'

But you can't fool all of the people all of the time, and particularly today, those who are not part of this compromised clerical system, and even some who are, no longer confuse God or the church with the institution. The last illusions are being shattered, the promises have proved empty, as the guest chair in my study, repeatedly drenched with tears over the last ten years, would testify if it could speak. But the sad fact is that there are laypeople still under the illusion that clergy want their gifts; and some still equate God and the church with the institution, many of them women who are clamouring for ordination to something that is called 'priesthood' but which does not seem to resemble Christ's priesthood in any way.

The institution and the church are not coterminous, in fact, in these days they hardly relate at all. There is an unbridgeable abyss between them that only Christ can cross, and Christ can do so only if both sides are receptive and responsive; much of the clericus seems not to be. Both sides are composed of people, but one side is composed of those who are entering the peace of Christ, who try to listen to something other than the ceaseless ranting of their own egos. It will be on account of their faithfulness that Christianity will survive even if, or perhaps because of, the demise of the present institutional clerical system. Christianity will renew itself in every generation.

There are hard things in this paper that must be said so that they can be consciously acknowledged and repented of in order to prepare the way for true change. We are at a watershed in history, and it is not axiomatic for the institution any more than for an individual that the church must endlessly repeat its destructive cycles. The essential question is not the ordination of women, but how ordination in itself has affected every area of Christian life. To focus this question, I will make a few remarks about the state of institutional churches in specific areas. Next, the overriding pathology of clericalism and its effects on liturgy, theology, and 'spirituality'. Lastly, to give some idea of what may lie ahead, a look at the American experience. These remarks are meant to provoke questions, not answer them. Some of what I say may seem unfair, but I have been asked to write from my own position and experience, which is not only that of a contemplative religious, but also that of many, many other women and men throughout Britain and America. Unlike much other writing on this subject, these remarks do not issue from a state of idealized wishful thinking and denial. First then, my own position.

*

My position: I dearly wish that the legislation allowing women to be ordained in the Church of England had been uncompromising. I devoutly wish even more, now that it has been passed, that women would refuse to be ordained into the clerical club and the system as it now stands in utter contradiction (as opposed to participating in the paradox of power in weakness) to the Christ whom it claims to serve, lest they, too, become corrupted, however they may vow to 'change the system from within'. For if one lies down with dogs, it is virtually impossible not to acquire their fleas.

And in this instance the fleas are what the desert mothers and fathers recognized as uncontrolled passions, subtle, strong, ravenous drives, the demons of Power, Pretension, Presumption, Pomposity, Privilege, Preferment and Patronage, which seven Ps are the modern versions of what the desert hermits named greed, unchastity, avarice, anger, melancholy, accedie, vainglory and pride, which later became known as the seven deadly sins.[6] The contemplative peace they sought, *apatheia*, which is the call of every Christian, was not repression of these passions (at which the male clericus seems particularly adept) but their harmonization, by being brought to focus on God alone.

My position: I hope to suggest how and why the only way forward is the de-institutionalization of the clergy. This would include lay presidency of the Eucharist, a situation no less catholic nor apostolic than the system we have now, because the apostolic lineage is conferred through baptism.[7] And I use the present tense because eucharistic communities are arising across the spectrum, from Catholic to Baptist—indeed the age of denominational barriers is over, whether the hierarchies care to acknowledge it or not. There is, today, a greater ecumenical church centred on the Eucharist that knows no boundaries, harking back to Christian origins. The richness of each tradition, the contribution each has to make, and the need for diversity has never been more apparent or more appreciated in helping everyone who will to listen to the Spirit. And through this appreciation has come the realization that barriers between denominations arise from those same uncontrolled or repressed passions that have created the *reductio ad absurdum* in which much institutional religion, of whatever stripe, today finds itself.

My position: when I thought there was still hope for the institution, that the clericalized could listen, I was angry (do not

confuse direct speech—truth-saying—by a woman, with anger[8]).
I grieved for the loss of great beauty,[9] of a spiritual culture, of
the wondrous mystery conveyed through the best of sacramental
theology, as I watched its transmission become increasingly frag-
mented, corrupted, fossilized, and bent to abusive use. Those
who deliberately have distorted it to their own exploitive ends
have been too lazy or cowardly or arrogant to undergo the icono-
clastic journey into the depths of God, indwelling beyond all
images, a journey that requires total denudation of the tomfoolery
of so-called self-image, a journey into the mystery of the resurrection, which is the heart of every Christian's vocation. Now I
believe the sooner the clerical institutions in their present form
collapse the better. I still have hope, but it lies elsewhere, as I
will describe.

My position: I am one of the marginalized; I avoid the institution
as much as I possibly can.[10] Years ago I stopped wearing my
habit in public, but the debate before the 1992 vote was so
vicious that I stopped wearing it entirely, not wanting in any way
to be identified, even mistakenly, with the clericus. Even the
Eucharist became politicized. Going to Communion became a
political act. I stopped going to Communion months before the
vote. I could not have coped both with the defeat of the measure
(which would have declared women something less than human
and questioned Christ's indwelling, *capax Dei*, supported the
institution's completely specious claims and its pathological desire
to control God), in combination with refraining indefinitely from
Communion should it have failed. Even so, given the circumstances of the debate on all sides, to go to Communion seemed
blasphemous. I continued to fast from Communion until Christmas out of sorrow.

These days I go to the Eucharist if I can find a celebrant
whose body language and vibes do not reek so much of the seven
devils that they reawaken the anger and pain I have fought so
hard to relinquish into the love of Christ for the sake of contemplating him alone, however badly I fail.[11] I go to beg my daily
bread and to pray that Mercy will, in the mystery of love, make
my 'soul and body a living sacrifice' in deed. Prayer and the
Christian journey are subject to universal laws. Every life presents

a moment, different for each person, at which one must choose between the activity of so-called morality (for example, fighting the street battles of church politics and women's rights), and contemplative stillness, the reciprocity of God's beholding, from which alone any true change can arise. I have long since made this choice.

But I also have come to know my own weaknesses, and am vigilant for dangerous situations. (Writing this paper is one of these, but for once I must take the risk.) Often I will come to church late and leave early. 'Eat and run' we used to call it. Not a bad policy. The desert mothers and fathers said 'flee bishops', considering that one of the most serious temptations was wanting to be ordained or fantasizing about it. I say this as one who was first offered ordination in the early sixties. I realized then, and the experience of the intervening thirty years has confirmed, that to accept ordination would compromise the priestly character of my solitary vocation, of any vocation, of the human condition. The essence of priesthood is the plunge into God's self-outpouring, the willingness to 'quit oneself as initiator and base of attitude and act and plunge into the act by which God wills and creates what is, *in willing himself.* By willing God, in this concrete context, we will all that is, not as we perceive it to be, but as God wills it to be and how he wills it to be in the mystery of his wisdom and love ... To which must be added that this willing is something that God does or is in us.'[12]

My position: I have none, not in this world. As such, I cannot but bear in the eyes of the fearful the terrible power of Christ's poor ones, who cannot be coerced or controlled, and who seek neither to coerce nor to control, but to adore. However badly I may fail in human eyes, I want to live for God alone, in Christ, as Eucharist, 'a holocaust for your people ...' was the way my profession put it. I wish to live, by grace, in every moment, so completely at the heart of this Eucharist that it would be a grave failure to step back far enough even to make the gestures of offering.

So much for my position.

Discerning the vision of God

With the institution's failure of vision has come the failure of discernment. While many women seeking ordination are driven by their uncontrolled passions, by the seven devils, others, now ordained deacon or seeking ordination, are distinctly uncomfortable with the system into which they are being forced and the process of discernment they have undergone. They quite rightly suspect, though they may not be able to articulate it, that they are making a Faustian covenant. They realize that fundamental questions have not been addressed, not just those of sex and power and pathology in the culturally compromised institution, but the much more fundamental questions of a single-hearted pursuit of the vision of God, of putting on the kenotic mind of Christ, which is the only source of any non-destructive 'good works' that might be done.[13]

These women realize that the freedom of Christ's promises has been turned on its head to become rigid categorization and conformity, the creature of class and status. Some are aware, quite conscious even, that theirs is a contemplative vocation, but since the church has no use for contemplation and will not support it no matter how piously it blathers about 'prayer', they perceive that the only way for them to survive physically is to become ordained. Contemplatives who follow a vision, who are compelled to follow it by the mind of Christ, do not do well in the dog-eat-dog, cut and thrust of the church of post-Thatcherite Britain or post-Reagan America. Women who have chosen the clergy option out of despair fail to realize that unless they are exceptionally lucky, the clergy club and the laity who decorate their own egos by acting as its minions, will eat them for breakfast.

What will happen to the anger of these women? Will it continue as depression in such a way that women, too, become part of the so-called ministry to women, exercised by males for centuries, a 'ministry' that simply feeds, feeds on, and perpetuates the hopeless closed world of their depression? For compassionate ministry is not the iron control of managed niceness and conformity with the status quo. And this sort of depression—I say this as one who knows from the inside—is often a form of accedie. Compassion is rather to help someone grow into the vision of God, and *metanoia* cannot take place until reality is faced, and depression broken. So often I want to say to these women, wake *up*! Get a life!

But before going further, let us look at what we know about the sort of God who gives the vision and what people must do to dispose themselves to receive it. Christianity was originally a vision that was communicated more by intuition and example than by speech.[14] It still is. It was the religion of the poor and poor-pure in heart. It still is. Christ's peace was fundamentally simple. It still is.[15] And we are all called to the same degree of union with God.

What sort of God are we talking about? The essence of God revealed in Christ is inexhaustible, self-emptying love (Phil 2.5–11). Christ comes to free us from slavery to the fear of death (Heb 2.14ff.) and to transfigure us into himself (see the gospel of John).[16] This Christ indwells us by the Spirit, bearing us to the Father. That is, God indwells us, and when we try to love purely, simply, in single-hearted self-forgetfulness, we are participating—a much more profoundly nuanced word than modern usage suggests—in divinity.

The New Testament is a continuation of the struggle of the Hebrew peoples, from Exodus through the prophets, to purify their own vision. 'I despise your sacrifices . . .' (Isaiah 1.11ff.). The Lord demands a pure and faithful heart; faithful, though all visible signs may seem so much folly. Who will see this invisible vision? It is given to those who go, or are driven, beyond all signs and signification into the far reaches of faith: to those who 'know their need of God' (the NEB redeems itself here), to the pure in heart, to the merciful, to the meek, to those who mourn from abuse or repentance or who weep for joy of the divine beauty, to those who hunger and thirst for righteousness, to the peacemakers, to the persecuted. To the Mary Magdalenes who, conflated into the single figure that is transmitted through tradition,[17] has been cured of the seven devils and all her other sins simply because 'she loved much'. She is the first to see the risen Christ—and of course the men, already caught in a cycle of pretension, and in a culture that despises women, will not believe her. In other words, those who are given the vision are

those (no matter what their station, for Kings have seen it as
well as the poor woman, Mary, from Nazareth) who are willing
to give up all wordly values in order to be plunged into divine
Love, to let Love have its way with them.

> Do not set your hearts on the world or what is in it. Anyone
> who loves the world does not love the Father. Everything in
> the world, all that panders to the appetites or entices the eyes,
> all the arrogance based on wealth, these spring not from the
> Father but from the world. That world with all its allurements
> is passing away, but those who do God's will remain for ever.
>
> (John 2.15–17)[18]

Institutional contradictions

In the light of these observations, the contradictions (not
paradoxes) inherent in the present situation are untenable. Here
are a few more:

— In Christ, both sacrifice (self-emptying) and priest (the
  will and gift to manifest this self-emptying) are
  indistinguishable. Why then do we create a duality?

— This sacrifice is made in the solitude of every human heart,
  and the body is the altar on which the Eucharist of each
  human life is made. Why then do we continue to allow
  the exaltation of one group of human beings to the
  denigration of others? What has happened to wonder, awe,
  reverence, before the unique mystery of each human
  person in whom God dwells in Christ by the spirit? And,
  by extension, before the unique mystery of creation?

— The purpose of Christian life is to realize our inherent
  gift of participation in God by becoming other Christs.
  Why do we imply that the ordained are more 'Christ' than
  the non-ordained?

— The Holy Spirit blows where she will, bestowing her
  charisms on the just and the unjust, but she unfailingly
  bestows grace through those who humbly wait on her, who,
  in attentive receptivity, are emptied of their self-
  preoccupation and drawn, in Christ, to the Father.

— Christ refused the temptation in the desert, and continued to refuse throughout his life, to lay claim, to grasp, equality with God (Phil 2.5–11). The Eucharist is the sacrament of his life. Why then do clerics and would-be clerics presume to 'claim' the Eucharist? Eucharistic celebration is not a 'right', nor a 'call', nor an 'exercise of power', nor cause for preferment. Life in Christ operates on the law of *un*grasping, the principle that humility *is* divinity, which has its corollary in the law of the paradox of intention, the fundamental law of prayer.[19] It is the life of one who is the most humble servant of all.

— The Church of England and Anglicanism in general has not become inculturated, it has become acculturated, compromised, corrupted by the very values the Christian vision opposes. Clergy no longer seem to be accountable beyond themselves. In Britain, this acculturation is tied up with Establishment; in America, with the deliberate adoption, fifty years ago, of a business model for the church. Nothing could have been more destructive or self-refuting. Acculturation is always a problem, but today there seems to be a total lack of discernment between the two, and claims of inculturation are used to justify acculturation, or hedonism, or, worst of all, 'human nature', which is a slur on the divine image and the true greatness of which human beings are potentially capable. While it could be argued that people have always used the church to further their own power, this does not make it right or necessary, and things certainly do not have to be as bad as they are at this time.

— Religious orders also are dying.[20] This is a pity because, if nothing else, they could provide a counterpole to market 'spirituality'. Having done exemplary work for years, they are affected by the same diseases as the rest of the church and society. They are dying from all the ills cited above and a few that are peculiar to themselves. They are not dying from lack of vocations: there are many thousands of vocations, but these vocations need simplicity, the basics, wise discernment, and thus have nowhere to go.

Like Christianity itself, Christian religious life, specifically monastic life, began as a lay movement.

Benedict himself was a layman. Yet religious life, like
Christianity, became clericalized within three centuries.
It is arguable that any sort of clericalization leads inevitably
to decline. The ordination of women may hasten or slow
the process of dying in women's communities. One of the
best-kept secrets in male communities[21] is the underlying
animosity between the ordained and the non-ordained.
With the clericalization of the self-image of religious
orders (a contradiction in terms), and the greater freedom
men superficially appear to be able to give one another,
it is a problem rarely voiced and often squelched. Male
bonding and all that. The ordained, after all, run the
communities. The lay brothers—well, ask them.

This situation gets even more interesting as women's
communities try to decide whether to admit ordained
women or whether to allow any of their own members to
be ordained. Women seem to have a greater need for
everyone to be alike, caused in part by their second-class
status in church and society. Competitive envy is
rampant.[22] One can only hope that communities will
awaken to the realization of how deeply infected they are
by the pathology of clericalism. After ten years in England
I still find it difficult to watch what British women,
especially in the church, put up with from men. Perhaps
they feel denial is the only way they can survive. But it
is deadly for both men and women.

— The nature of theological debate at the official level
throughout modern Christendom reeks of presumption,
i.e., imposed, arrogant ignorance. Some of those involved
still operate on a so-called 'natural law' that has little to
do with the way we now know that God in fact makes the
creation (attitudes towards women and homosexuals, for
example), and even less with Christology. Others presume
to know what God thinks and what makes people tick, as
if they were psycho-biological or theological-ethical
machines stamped to a universal template. There are
universal laws, but they work from within, not from
without. These people seem unable to comprehend that
by condemning parts of creation, they are condemning

God who made it as it is. Whatever happened to humility
before the mystery? To faith in search of understanding?
— Domestication, recent scientific studies tell us, whether the
co-domestication of animals and humans, or human
attempts to domesticate God, leads only to the behavioural
regression of the parties involved, and, in the latter case,
the trivialization of God by religion. One does not have to
look far among the clergy to see infantile behaviour.

It does not take a theologian—many theologians would be the
last to be able to perceive them—to see that life in Christ and
the concrete situation among Church of England leaders (as
opposed to their public pronouncements) are completely at odds.
It almost seems as if we have entered the phase of life in an
organism where the body is killed and only the sickness, which
has destroyed it, remains, having, in the process, condemned
itself. It is also a commonplace that organizations have a terminal
phase in which those who are less healthy and more oblivious
retain control and drive the more healthy and visionary away.

The foregoing does not bode well for women coming into the
clerical system. And from what I have seen in America as well
as Britain, the women being ordained are becoming even more
clericalized than the men, perhaps because they are the new kids
on the block and less secure, like any convert, over-zealous and
anxious to toe the party line. At the same time, many of them
are distinctly uncomfortable, often bearing a deep and undifferen-
tiated unease, a sense that they are betraying something.

How, under these circumstances, women will be able to turn
the tide I do not know and I do not think they know, either.
Certainly the faces on television in November 1992 were not
encouraging, nor have been subsequent encounters with women
clergy.[23] And the question has to be asked if they are not wasting
their time (as well as selling their souls) by entering such a
moribund system in the first place?

The only potentially hopeful sign I see at the moment is the
financial disaster on the Church Commissioners' desks. Lack of
finance may force the Church of England to redefine what it
means by ministry, and to ask what is worth supporting. However,
given its history, and the amount of self-interested scrambling

that will perhaps inevitably take place among the people who will
be making these decisions, it is perhaps more realistic to regard
this potential hope as wishful thinking.

There is the additional problem that people in the Church of
England appear to go to church for many disparate reasons, often
social ones, to engage in what might irreverently be called 'tea
party religion'. Without excluding this valid and useful social
activity, the Church of England must decide what its *principal*
function and purpose really is, from which all else must proceed.
It must prioritize.

Is this governing principle to keep the comfortable cosy, using
the model of the vestigial and often mythical country parish?
(Which is not to say that there are not remarkable and healthy
country parishes.) To be the ritual arm of the state, and cere-
monial resource for the world (for all the world knows that no
one does liturgy better than the C of E at its best)? To be a
political pressure group? To be a moral force (though its credibility in this area, especially after the ordination debate, is deeply
in doubt)? To be a colourful tourist attraction (it has been
observed that it does some of its best work simply by keeping
the cathedrals open and not bothering the millions of tourists
who in some mysterious way find God in them—which is not to
say that there are not cathedrals that are real centres of prayer)?

Or is it to bear the vision so that the people do not perish?—
Which means back to the drawing board.

Clericalism

I have used the word 'pathology' a lot in this chapter. Clericalism
(as distinct from the people it destroys) is a kind of contagious
sickness. It is inherent in a hierarchical system. It infects clergy
without distinction and without their knowing. It sets them apart
as a class, which is a very different matter from the setting-
apart of holiness that indwells the interior solitude of each human
being. Clericalism is inherently destructive, both to the person
who is already infected and to those affected, and therefore often
infected, by that person's life; it perpetuates the classic co-
dependent cycle and its denial.

It is denial that makes clericalism intrinsically abusive to others.[24] It gives the impression of sacramentalizing the seven devils: Power, Pretension, Presumption, Pomposity, Privilege, Preferment and Patronage. Clericalism is doubly destructive in that it reinforces the abuse people receive from an increasingly violent culture, which they bring to the Eucharist to be healed. Clericalism traps them in a depressive self-consciousness that is one of the most subtle and pernicious effects of any sort of abuse, and is the opposite of the freedom from self-consciousness that is called 'salvation'.

Clericalism is a collusion among those who deliberately choose to be deaf and blind especially to themselves (John 9). It arises from a need to hide: to hide from oneself, which gives the illusion of hiding from other people. The need to hide is itself pathological. Clericalism creates a Dives and Lazarus abyss. There is no way to cross it. Even supposedly well-intentioned groups such as Affirming Catholicism 'forgot' (I quote two of the organizers) to invite the laity to its initial meeting, and seems merely to be yet another mask behind which the old evils hide themselves.

Sometimes clericalism takes the form of clergy creating problems or eliciting them from people so that they, the clergy, will have someone to 'help' and can thereby feed their egos on another's suffering. Some clergy have a genius for tapping into other people's most vulnerable spots and throwing them off balance into dependence. Sometimes clericalism, especially when it is linked to sexual problems, takes the form of excessive devotion to Mary with its consequent hatred of flesh-and-blood women. Sometimes sexual problems are expressed in excessive, even compulsive, concern with ritual. The variations are endless.

Clericalism like other forms of addiction always needs a bigger fix. Witness the history of orders in the church. Witness the ecumenical dialogue conducted at the official level where the power stakes are highest, a dialogue that without question accepts claims that appear to have little foundation in fact for which there is scholarly evidence.

The problem is that clericalism creates a Girardian spiral:[25] when the abused take power, they become the abusers. In a society where women are held in contempt by men, women cannot but have contempt for each other. When they have had all the ground on which they might stand taken from them, they will try to take from each other the little scrap another might have in order to have the illusion of a slightly surer footing. And when women take power, they have exactly the same potential for abuse of others as men do. The men, of course, often say they have been abused by women.

Liturgy

Fundamental prayer is simple with the simplicity of convergence; so is liturgy: Christ presides in the midst of the assembly, his Body, when two or three are gathered together. It is in his presence that the liturgy is celebrated. The self-effacement of all concerned, the degree to which liturgical action effaces itself, gestures towards a present union with Christ in the eternal liturgy.

For a church that has a reputation for splendid liturgy, the Church of England's Alternative Service Book was a rude shock. Banal and prolix, especially limp, verbose and distracting at the climax of the Eucharist, the Fraction,[26] whose significance is lost, it is like the proverbial camel designed by a committee, one that could have been produced only by a clericalized hierarchical system.

We need good liturgy. We need many different kinds of liturgies. We need liturgies that are simple and silent, and liturgies that are splendid with all the stops pulled out, but which also are full of silence (we do not, however, need the clericalism that usually is the price of such liturgies). It doesn't matter which way the celebrant faces; it doesn't matter which way the people face.

What matters is that the words and signs efface themselves so that the worshipper is conveyed into the ineffable where both individual and neighbour, solitude and communion are found in union in God.[27] All useful sacred signs efface themselves, even the Eucharist itself: at the Fraction, the Bread is held up and broken to reveal the emptiness that lies between its two halves, the ineffable from which fullness of life is returned. This gesture recalls the holy of holies, the empty tomb, and mirrors the dynamic by which humans pray, the grace of self-forgetfulness by which they become transfigured, the relinquishing of thoughts and self-concern into silence, and the emergence of new life from that Silence. The Fraction is visceral action: God gives himself into our hands and our lives to be broken.[28]

What matters is that entertainment and performance are not mistaken for worship; too much importance is focused on celebrants. In the liturgy, Christ is giving Christ to himself. Instead of pointing to themselves, celebrants need to know how to efface themselves in order to point to the Christ whose self-effacing presence is made manifest. And the priestly charism (rarely found amongst the ordained, in my experience) is, once again, to plunge into God's self-outpouring, the willingness to 'quit oneself as initiator and base of attitude and act and plunge into the act by which God wills and creates what is, *in willing Himself* . . . this willing is something that God does or is in us.' It is the ability in some way to express and/or manifest for others what they are unable to, while simultaneously disappearing.[29] To disappear even as the manifestation is given, which allows it to bypass the discursive mind, to plunge into and enhance the self-outpouring of the worshipping heart. In this the celebrant becomes both sacrifice (self-effacement) and priest (taking on the burden of others' self-consciousness in order to help them express their pain/joy), and this gift comes *only* to, and through, the poor-pure in heart.

This means that in any given situation the same person may not be the person to preside at the Eucharist on all occasions because no one is consistently pure-poor in heart, and no one person can be inspired with the appropriate expression for every situation. This means that if the community has to discern who is the appropriate person to preside at the Eucharist on any particular occasion, its members will be required to listen to each other in a different way: each becomes a potential God-bearer for the group. The priestly charism cannot be taught; it is a gift. It can be faked, but it will turn on, and eventually destroy the faker.

One senses at least two motives behind the doctrine of *ex opere*: a profound exasperation that attempts to shut its eyes and bypass the problem, retreating into God's inviolable mercy, and an invitation to license by abstracting, fragmenting and compartmentalizing incarnational theology. '*Ex opere* fails to take into consideration the profound impact of psychological signals vital to the transformational context of the liturgy.'[30] While the operation of grace in itself may be unaffected in a purely abstract, artificial and disincarnate world, the ability to *receive* grace, which is always co-operative, may be profoundly impaired, especially by invasive, unspoken signals coming from a self-serving celebrant, given that the liturgy dissolves distinctions between outside and inside, thus bringing the context of the liturgy *within* the worshipper. Grace is inherently relational.

Theology

Clericalism is rife because theological education makes it so. Clericalism follows the fault line of the split that took place in the seventeenth century between 'academic' theology and practical training (the latter being much despised). The split continues to this day. Academic theology in its present form, long waltzing with the 'dying bride of German rationalism' is, now, with her, at the end.[31] In England the trends leading towards the death of theology are summarized by the work of Richard Swinburne. The irony of this situation is that many of the breakthroughs in understanding language (the so-called post-modern movement) were begun by logical positivists, yet while language studies have not only flourished but also given us new and better tools for studying mystical texts, the heirs of the positivists, confined to abstract mind games and linearity, have reached *reductio ad absurdum*. As Niels Bohr said to Albert Einstein, 'You are not thinking, you are merely being logical.'

We live in a multivalent and interrelated world, something the ancients well understood. The message of the gospels is conveyed in paradoxes. Paradoxes are not botched premises that need dismantling and explaining. They are descriptors: they describe something empirical that cannot be described any other way, and it is only by going through the gates of paradox that the empirical will be discovered.[32] To think using the tools of paradox is much more difficult than mere linearity. It is not that logic is abandoned, for in the thought-clusters of this multivalent universe descriptive logic becomes much more precise, in part because a multivalent universe is not being forced into univalence.

Academic theology is the last bastion of a kind of scientism that scientists, in the wake of Einstein, Heisenberg, Bell and Bohm, have long since abandoned. Indeed, science is itself primarily a language.[33] Theology is not done in a vacuum: every statement has psycho-spiritual, moral and sociological nuances. Yet from all appearances, Church of England ordinands have far too little formal training in pastoral care. What there is often appears to be regarded as merely 'doing time'. They do not seem to learn how to connect real life and theory/theology—to American eyes, a typical example of the 'minds cut off from bodies' syndrome. Their training does not appear to include basic counselling skills. There seems to be no equivalent to the obligatory Clinical Pastoral Education[34] mandatory for ordinands in virtually all denominations in the USA, *in addition to* field work placements in *each* of three years of theological education. There appears to be no process by which ordinands can learn how their own problems might affect their work with others. Rather, ordinands seem to be taught how to hide these problems under the veneer of a clerical mask. The sort of education American ordinands receive hasn't made an obvious difference in the fate of American churches (although it has improved the quality of ministry), but it gives them less excuse.

However, even laudable programmes have a way of being co-opted into and compromised by clericalism. An American friend writes, 'CPE [is] turning into another power ploy instead of the adventure in self-awareness it was *supposed* to be and formation contradictions—like theological students being *required* to have a spiritual director who is *registered* with the Dean of Ordinands ... so that the training people can write to the director about problems they see in the student. Talk about boundary violations!'

To the outsider, impressions of ordinands' public conversations and behaviour range from the comical to the revolting. There was the day that two were seated across the aisle on the London bus. That peculiarly smug, priggish, slightly fatuous expression of complacency and privilege I associate with Anglo-Catholicism was already firmly imprinted on their faces. They were ostentatiously reading breviaries. Their ridiculous behaviour might be dismissed as children's play if the consequences of clericalism were not so deadly; clergy have a way of not growing up. Another day I overheard a conversation between two presumptive high-fliers who were complaining about the amount of time they had to 'waste' putting up with people in their field-work parishes. And there are those with the agendas from whom I cannot run fast enough, with their fixed smiles and closed minds. These are subjective impressions, the sort of impressions the non–church-goer might have, however unrepresentative they may be; but then, I was asked to write a subjective paper, and I am not alone in this perspective.

'Spirituality'

There is nothing so simple as prayer and the journey into God. One needs but to sit in stillness with an open heart. The rest is sheer gift, the grace of Love alone.

Prayer is the mystery of the resurrection by which we are drawn to the Father.

Modern advances in psychology have helped us better to understand what happens in our interior silence, but psychology is no substitute for still-prayer. One thing that has come clear is that we have to know enough of the truth of our selves[35] to have an unfolding truth to give to God. The truth of our self is continually emerging from silence and cannot be categorized; it is not the ego, or the much-vaunted self-image, which is primarily an illusory fantasy construction of a personality in search of itself. And the silence has to be fed, carefully, for in the silence, nothing is eliminated or left behind. 'Our past goes before us', as St Augustine (much misunderstood and fashionably maligned) observed.

Yet there is nothing so difficult as this still-prayer, for it requires that we relinquish our wilfulness. We are always devising ways wilfully to distract ourselves from the sometimes frightening confrontation with the holy, and the willingly docile receptivity required to receive it. Distraction which contemporary so-called spirituality provides in vast amounts. The 'spirituality' fad is riding the Thatcherite wave. It has become a market commodity and has created a 'priesthood' and clericalism of its own.[36]

The commodity mentality is evidenced by the occasional visitor, always someone I have never seen before, who comes into my study, sits down, and starts talking, can't stop talking, talking without a break about this programme and that, Jung, Myers-Briggs, Ignatian spirituality, enneagrams, pilgrimages, the newest form of therapy . . . I wait in silence, not that I could stem the flood even if I wanted to. Often the person is badly in need of basic psychotherapy. Usually the person has had a genuine glimpse of God, but has been fruitlessly searching for the 'right' way to go about pursuing it (the slot syndrome again). Usually the person is deeply angry, 'angry unto death' (Jonah 4.9), and angry at the time and, frequently, the large sums of money they feel they have wasted, realizing at some level that something basic is missing and has never been addressed.[37]

We live not in the New Age but in the new age of empire-building celebrity gurus, spiritual technology and commodity 'spirituality'.[38] Who was it who said that con artists succeed because in their heart of hearts people want to be fooled? A close look at some of these movements reveals further evidence of control. More than one Roman Catholic friend of mind (including a Jesuit) agrees that it is worrying to realize that St Ignatius emerged in the Counter-Reformation and that so-called Ignatian spirituality is being revived under the present pontiff.

Similarly, behind the somewhat dubious claims of techniques such as the Myers-Briggs inventory are yet more tools of 'spiritual' control. Such strategies simply put people more firmly in their slots, and amplify an erroneous impression of 'normal', which in its deep sense means not 'according to a universal standard' but rather 'true to type'. Most of what goes on in the 'spirituality' movement appeals to the desire for a quick fix and the narcissistic pleasures of watching oneself be a 'mystic', which amounts to little more than additional distraction and further layers of self-consciousness. When added to the problematic British penchant for acting, an individual's spiritual dilemma can seem byzantine. Much of it carries the loaded message of the self-help movement that there is always something more wrong with us that needs to be fixed—by us. Only God can effect the

grace of transfiguration. Whatever made us presume to manipu-
late the holy? Whatever happened to the mystery of the human
person, whose simple gaze on God can be more healing than
years with a psychotherapist? Whatever happened to 'sit in your
cell and your cell will teach you everything'?

Which is not to say that psychotherapy does not have its place.
But in the last ten years psychotherapy seems to have abandoned
its brief of helping people to recognize the truth of the self, of
helping them towards maturity, which includes, among other
criteria, the ability to postpone gratification and the ability to
live with ambiguity. Psychotherapy (over 400 psychotherapies at
last count—makes you wonder) also has joined the commodity
market. This is especially true in the United States. In Britain,
psychotherapy seems more like drip feed, and the subtext is that
if you have let the side down enough to ask for help, then, bad
luck, you're a write-off. From an American perspective, British
psychotherapy seems divided into schools that vaguely resemble
the cultish groups one associates with Glastonbury. In addition,
the few British psychotherapists I have met seem very much *de
haut en bas*, which is not encouraging. I must admit that my
point of view is influenced by the stories of the people who sit
in the tear-drenched guest chair, and that I exaggerate (but only
a little) to make a point.

To each their own poison, but, whatever it is, the subtext,
once again, is control. So-called lay ministry, especially when it
takes the form of that loathsome phrase 'spiritual direction' can
quickly degenerate into admission to the foyer of the clerical
club, glamour and power by association. No degree or course of
instruction can create a spiritual person, or a person capable
of discernment.

> The life of prayer entails going beyond without end, a refusal
> to rest content, a thirst for the infinite that shatters the pious,
> safe idols we are endlessly making one after another. This is the
> desert.
>
> It is possible to live for years alone in a cell, occupied solely
> with the things of God, without even passing the threshold of
> solitude, for want of leaving an infantile world peopled with
> images, 'spiritual' pleasures, and words without end. An entire
> world that reflects only the multiple facets of our own self and

our unconscious desires. It is this self that one risks adoring,
and not God. We need images, sensibility, concepts, but we
must know how to go beyond, to leave the surface to plunge
into the silence of faith, the humility of solitude, the boundless
infinity of Love.

Get behind me, Satan! Our thoughts are not God's thoughts.

The way of faith is a Way that is not a way. It is the mysterious
world of the resurrection. It is Christ, his death and his life.
It is the Spirit who blows where it will. It is the Father whose
infinite love cannot ever be circumscribed. Let us leave our selves
to be borne by the Spirit towards the Father, ever renewing our
abandonment in Christ.

> We know that the Son of God has come and has given us
> understanding so that we may know him who is true, and
> we are in him who is true, in his Son Jesus Christ. He is
> the true God and eternal life. Little children, keep
> yourselves from idols.
>
> (1 John 5.20–21)[39]

The American experience

To have some idea of what ordination of women may mean for
the future, it is useful to look at the American experience.

In response to an invitation to pursue research, I left America
nearly ten years ago. I have great love and respect for my adopted
country, enough to observe it closely, if not uncritically. If I
preferred the USA I would live there. I go back every year
partly for family and business reasons, partly out of horrified
fascination, and mainly to have solitude in the Alaska wilderness.
In the past ten years, I have watched the situation in ECUSA
(Episcopal Church in the USA) continue to deteriorate. That
women have been ordained for fifteen years or so is merely
incidental to this process of decline, which has been going on
for at least half a century.

Around the time women were first ordained in the USA, there
began a mad general rush for ordination. There were a lot of
reasons given, personal call (always questionable and rarely properly discerned); desire to celebrate the Eucharist (subtext: a weak
personality, that is, inchoate, unintegrated, seeking a form
exterior to itself by acquiring personal power over others); gifts

that 'must be shared [read forced on] with the [poor benighted] people'; 'worker priest'; and the most distorting of all, a reason I have often heard voiced in Britain as well, that one is not really a 'complete' Christian until one is ordained.[40] The selection process in ECUSA is slightly different in each diocese, but it is so haphazard, and relies so thoroughly on American self-promotion and sales ability, that the people who perhaps might be bearers of 'the vision' and able to convey it either don't bother to apply or are turned down.

If you look at the American 'Red Book' or at ECUSA's equivalent of Crockford's (which goes by a slang name too vulgar to print in a respectable English volume on religion), what is immediately noticeable is that in many dioceses there are twice, even three times as many non-stipendiary clergy as there are stipendiary. They predictably cluster around the richest areas of the country. There appears to be a geographical parallel among non-stipendiary clergy in England, although, at least until recently, these were usually ordained for entirely different (and equally questionable) reasons than their American cousins.

In ECUSA, the clergy glut is so great (and the quality often so appalling) that some dioceses have now put a moratorium on ordinations. There are so many clergy in some parishes that at an early service there will be more clergy in the sanctuary than worshippers in the pews. ECUSA is arguably one of the most clericalized churches in the world. It has reached the point that when I am in the USA I go to one or two ECUSA services in a vain search for signs of hope, and the rest of the time go to Roman Catholic Mass. A lot of people do this, and the traffic is both ways. As a Catholic friend of mine, who goes to an ECUSA parish, says, 'I can pray there. It's not my politics. I can leave politics behind.'

The promise of new vision and a new church associated with having ordained women has not materialized in ECUSA. In fact, the women seem more and more to be adopting the 'executive' model, and they dress like upper-level management cum dog collars. Or perhaps they have opted for the earth mother/goddess model. Whatever, when I see one of these assertive types coming—the attitude is set in the face—I run (some things are identical on both sides of the Pond). I have come to dread clergy (female or male) who come at me with an agenda more than those who try to degrade me by their élitism (male or female). This says something about me, of course. If I were utterly receptive to the vision of God I should not notice, for love does not take offence, and humility is not aware of injury. But I am weak, and I bear wounds I cannot afford to have reopened quite yet.

ECUSA is in a state of decline. The usual placebos of 'programme' are offered, but the subtext can no longer remain hidden: the clergy are the problem. There is also a financial crisis: people refuse to give money for the 'CEO's office' in New York, or for centralized programmes. Thus, proposals are being prepared for decentralization. However, it is questionable how effective any remedy will be because, as with the C of E, the basic issues have not been addressed, and the vision of God is virtually never mentioned.

For example, this past summer I was shown a draft document from a committee on the environment (first year's budget: $30,000). I have had lifelong involvement in ecological issues. This document was one of the few developments in ECUSA that prompted any curiosity. I read it, and handed it back to the member of Executive Council who had shown it to me. 'What's wrong?' he asked. I just looked at him, wondering how to put it. He is an old and dear friend.

Finally I said 'Where is there anything about repentance, especially repentance for presumption and exploitation, where is there anything about wonder, about humility before the mystery of creation? Where is that key Native American word, "respect"? Where is there mention of the vision of God from which any accurate perception of the interrelatedness of creation must arise? This document is entirely presumptuous.'

My friend was scribbling as I talked. He handed the document back. 'Where would you put such statements?' I did my own scribbling on the opening preamble, and the papers changed hands again, as I said 'There's no place here to put something in about the vision of God. This document should be redone from scratch.' 'There isn't time', my friend said, 'it has to be through the committee process for General Convention next year.' Then he looked at me: 'It would have been pretty futile to have put you on the committee, wouldn't it?' 'Yes', I responded, thinking how much ECUSA committees resemble the British syndrome of not really wanting to solve problems but merely talking about them endlessly.

'Futile.'

Trying to comfort me, my friend voiced what I had been thinking by saying 'Next year when I have all this bureaucracy out of the way, I'll try to get back to having something of a spiritual life.'

'Isn't that exactly backwards?'

But I didn't say it.

The American experience: having women at the altar is more or less routine now. Some of them still try too hard. Most have faded into the clerical landscape and are lost to the rest of us. Only the most conservative parishes and 'the Synod', an Anglo-Catholic rump, still make a fuss. No one pays much attention because the pathology is self-evident. What has not changed is discrimination. In fact, it is almost harder for women now that the law is in place. 'What are you complaining about?', a clergyman will say when discrimination is pointed out, 'women have equal rights under canon law.' But the law and its implementation, the changing of cultural perceptions, are two very different matters.

Some conclusions

The foregoing leads to some inexorable conclusions: we need to de-institutionalize the clergy.[41] The more prominent the clergy, the more clerical the church, the less the self-effacing, humble Christ is revealed. We need people to take care of buildings and administer funds and be points of focus, but they do not have to be ordained. We need to find means of regularly holding up the mirror of Christ's humility and self-outpouring love before each Christian, but most particularly before those in positions of leadership, who tend to lose their humanity.[42] This used to be the role of confession, but it, too, was destroyed by the abuse of power and the disease of clericalism. *Nepsis*, vigilance, was the watchword of the desert hermits against the seven devils: human beings do not have to be victims of their thoughts and impulses;

they do have to want to be free from this bondage, from their sloth and self-absorption.

We need most of all to stop thinking in dualistic terms of 'clerics', 'ministers' and 'laity' and think instead in terms of *persons* who have equal membership in the Body, to examine from scratch what we are in fact doing in the liturgy. The gifts of the Spirit are not magic, which is a function of the pathology of control; the gifts of the Spirit are as vast and free as God's immense love, and are given everywhere and to all, according to the individual capacity to receive. How to increase the capacity of each person to receive God's gifts is the primary teaching task of religious leaders, to teach themselves, first of all.

Sometimes the image arises of the wider institutional church as a person who sits in my tear-drenched guest chair. Shaking this off, I sometimes wish instead that I could write a letter to the churches, particularly to the Anglican Communion and the Roman Catholic Church. This is what I would say.

I would remind each person, ordained and baptized, that God loves every one as a dear child, that it is possible to rest and weep in the lap of God, who cradles us in the Holy Spirit, who, in her womb, can bring us to new birth in Christ, who bears us to the Father. If we would only be empty, we can be filled with God, and by this Love we would learn that being obedient is not as to a sovereign, but a response of love called out of us by One who continually pours out his life for us, and in us, as deep calls to deep, *kenosis* calls to *kenosis*. 'The God we pray to is always more humble than we are.' If we can only learn to be in the present moment, to 'will God' in the present moment of eternity, a present moment that requires no doing—we must be done with doing until the vision is restored. The vision of God's love from which the churches began, like Abraham's vision, changes even as we approach it, and will never desert us, not ever, no matter how we might feel inside, if only we will contemplate this immense, fathomless, enfolding humble Love, and listen to its voice.

Those of us who care deeply enough about the institution to risk criticizing it, who have risked so much for it, will not desert it, for we know that underneath the burnout there is still the inner ear to hear, the luminous eye to see, the heart to love, and the humility to forgive others, to forgive itself, and most of all, to receive God's loving forgiveness.

To will God. What does this mean?

A Carthusian describes it thus: 'To change something you must first will it, or rather will God in it.'

> The willing of what is, is, at once, utterly simple, yet very mysterious ... of the order of intuition and practice. One would perhaps go a step further and speak of willing *God* in a situation, rather than the situation with God. One would quit oneself as initiator and base of attitude and act and plunge into the act by which God wills and creates what is, *in willing Himself*. By willing God, in this concrete context, we will all that is, not as we perceive it to be, but as God wills it to be and how he wills it to be in the mystery of his wisdom and love ... To which must be added that this willing is something that God does or is in us.[43]

Fiat.

Postscript

The Church of England as an institution is dying. The ordination of women will not hasten that death, but in the present climate there is little reason to hope their ordination will arrest it. Perhaps *in extremis* the Church of England will be delivered from its devils; perhaps *in extremis* it will be able to receive deliverance into faith, silence and stillness; perhaps it will be given a near-death experience. In stillness, in the vision of God, there is neither up nor down, neither career success nor failure, no pinnacle and no long slide down from it. There is only the union of beholding and the action that issues from it (2 Cor 5.14).

It might be argued that this hope begs the question, but that is precisely the point: we are now beggars, or ought to be. We don't know what to do. Instead of making something up to make ourselves feel better, we need to wait and listen, without images and without plans, and, as anyone who truly prays will tell you, from this silence will be given more in concrete reality than we could possibly ask or imagine. But there must be faith, there must be patience, there must be willingness to 'will God', who is the source of all real vision and its working out in the nitty-gritty. Thus for me to make specific suggestions would be simply to set up a new set of stereotypes, a new set of slots for people to be crammed into; it would be to grasp at power; our only hope is to *un*grasp.[44]

I have written this chapter from the point of view of someone who has nothing to lose, to whom the institutional church on both sides of the Atlantic has done everything it is possible to do to a woman except take my life, and once or twice it has come pretty close to that.[45] Yet, without in any way caving in, I can say with Julian of Norwich, that this too can be turned to God's purpose, who saves his Word in all things; that, while injustice is never God's will, these 'harrowing' experiences have been woven into that holy will, which is perfect, that is to say, not static, but mature in its fullness. The insight that there is an immense love behind the universe is, as Helen Waddell observed, quoting Dante, initially a kind of outrage upon the soul. But as the gift of faith is given in the far reaches beyond all reason and understanding, it is the source of the only life worth having, an unspeakable solemn joy.

The grace to put on the kenotic, inviolably vulnerable mind of Christ, to adore, bestows on Christ's poor ones the joy no one and nothing can take from us, however badly we may fail. It is a freedom to which each human being is invited. It is not anarchy leading to the fascism in which individualism invariably ends, but solitude cultivated for the sake of community. It is not rebellion against authority, but surrender to the highest authority, responding with obedience to those who also seek the mind of Christ, the most humble servants of all, who therefore may be legitimate authorities (Phil 2.5–11). To choose otherwise would be to fail the temptation in the desert, to adore the Adversary in exchange for the sorry kingdoms of this world.

What I have learnt from all of this is the age-old lesson that people, however well-intentioned, will always fail. God, and the fathomless vision that God longs to give, will never fail. It requires only that we acknowledge the gift in utter gratitude by cooperation with the grace that enables our simplicity, that opens our hearts to God for God to enlarge and purify with the fire of love—God, whose thoughts and ways are not ours. Christ's peace is utterly simple, a simplicity that can never be comprehended, only received, and through it we are drawn into the mystery God's own self-outpouring, into speechless wonder and ineffable joy.

> They who wait for the Lord shall renew their strength,
>> they shall mount up with wings like eagles,
>>> they shall run and not be weary,
>>> they shall walk and not faint.[46]

Notes

1 I am writing two days after the James Bulger trial verdict. Morality, including, especially, the virtues of humility and truth, is not mere niceness in a subjunctive mode, 'Wouldn't it be nice if . . .'. As the Bible points out again and again, it is a matter of life and death. Morality is contingent on the vision of God and the fundamental process of prayer, whose laws I have described elsewhere: *they are universal laws.* The charge that the C of E is primarily concerned with fashionable causes such as South Africa and the homeless is apt, the former being international, and therefore glamorous, the latter safe and affecting, i.e., it makes the C of E look good both to itself and to others. While there are some dedicated people working on council estates, one wonders how many clergy really care to notice squalor, but prefer the image that appeared in the same time-frame as the Bulger trial verdict on the cover of a glossy magazine: a sporting cleric holding a hound. The issue here is not clergy in sport but the significance of the image: so concerned are clergy with image that they have tended to become caricatures of themselves. Rich or poor, sporting or sedentary, where there is no vision, and the laws of the mind which are included in the laws of prayer are not understood and practised, there can be no integrity lived or taught, and the people perish.

2 Perhaps following that of the scholar G. R. Driver, who makes a connection between the word 'vision' and the word 'magistrate'; cited in W. McKane, *Proverbs* (London: SCM, 1970). The verse is called 'obscure', and commentators puzzle over the shift in emphasis from community to individual. It is perhaps also significant that among these translations, it is only the British who opt for the authoritarian interpretation. An impeccable source tells me that the NEB is full of such 'Driverisms', i.e., far-fetched, and usually erroneous connections, and that the work of the REB has been in large part to eliminate them—that the REB scholars overlooked this one is perhaps a collective Freudian lapse.

3 See Isaiah 6.10. In the final stages of writing this article, arrangements with Rome for dissident Anglicans were announced, and on
the same day I came across 'The laity and the leadership crisis'
by Margaret O'Brien Steinfels in the Roman Catholic journal
Commonweal (10 September 1993). This article spookily echoes
everything I have written here, and particularly telling—especially
for those about to swim the Tiber—was this: 'These internal
problems are steadily exacerbated by resistance from Rome and a
growing paralysis among our bishops ... intellectually and spiri-
tually; literally unable ... to hear the voice of the people and to
read the signs of the time ... answering questions that no one is
asking, performing acts that no one understands.

'In that case, the actual task of maintaining Catholic identity
and salvaging a Catholic community will fall to lay people, even
though they remain second-class citizens in the church and far
removed from the sources of power and influence ...

'... lay Catholics have finally to grow up and assume their
responsibilities. The most active lay people have become complicit
in a kind of division of labor, agitating for change in the church
while leaving the job of maintaining continuity and personal and
institutional identity to clergy and bishops. Yet every passing year
makes it more unlikely that priests and bishops can carry out the
assignment to the extent required. This situation requires greater
cooperation and collaboration on the part of both sides; but lay
people cannot become mere deputies. They must show more
initiative and creativity ... the false divisions between lay people
who "work for the church" and those who "work in the world"
must be seen for what they are—false divisions ...

'I look at *Commonweal*, at NCR [*National Catholic Reporter*] ...
I think of Dorothy Day and the Catholic Worker. No one gave
permission and no one asked; the work was started and it has
continued.'

4 G. B. Shaw is more succinct: 'Every profession is a conspiracy
against the laity.' You cannot pay people to be self-emptying. The
corruption of leadership gives psychological permission for the
same behaviour to be repeated by others.

5 I make no apologies for using this metaphor for reasons that will
come clear.

6 Pride, covetousness, lust, envy, gluttony, anger, sloth. The seven
gifts of the Holy Ghost are wisdom, understanding, counsel, fortitude, knowledge, piety, fear of the Lord. The seven virtues are
faith, hope, charity, justice, prudence, temperance, fortitude. It is
not difficult to see which side of the balance the institution is on.

7 See Stephen Sykes, 'Vision and voting: reflections on the Anglican

doctrine of the Church' in *Living the Mystery* (London: Darton, Longman & Todd, 1994).

8 The British seem terrified of anger, which may be why they mistakenly see it everywhere, projecting it on to quite different human experiences such as pain, especially psycho-spiritual pain, fear, grief, and anguish, and especially on women, as accusation. See Walter Brueggemann, *Hopeful Imagination* (London: SCM, 1992). Straight talk is not popular in Britain, and is becoming less so in the USA. Without it, difficult situations become complex, desperate, dire, and finally terminal. Brueggemann points out that Jeremiah's passion is not anger but profound and terrible grief, and that it is only out of grief that newness can come. See my *The Fountain and the Furnace* (Mahwah: Paulist, 1987), for an explication of the psycho-spiritual dynamic at work.

9 See Hans Urs von Balthasar, *The Glory of the Lord*, vol. I (Edinburgh: T. & T. Clark, 1982).

10 This has nothing to do with the fact that I am a professed solitary. The solitary vocation is at the heart of the church, often visibly and actively so, depending on the nature of the individual solitary vocation, and the rhythms of the Spirit.

11 I am not passing judgement here: I am talking only about the impression celebrants may give; clergy are often so lacking in self-knowledge that they think their intention is what they are in fact communicating.

12 *The Way of Silent Love*, by A Carthusian, vol. III (London: Darton, Longman & Todd, forthcoming).

13 ' "But then," the boy said, frowning at the stars, "is the balance to be kept by doing nothing? Surely a man must act, even not knowing all the consequences of his act, if anything is to be done at all?"

' "Never fear. It is much easier for me to act than to refrain from acting . . . do nothing because it is righteous or praiseworthy or noble to do so; do nothing because it seems good to do so; do only that which you must do and which you cannot do in any other way." ' Ursula K. Le Guin, *The Farthest Shore* (New York: Bantam, 1969), p. 67.

14 See Aloys Grillmeier SJ, tr. John Bowden, *Christ in Christian Tradition*, vol. I (2nd edn; London: Mowbray, 1975), p. 35.

15 See *The Way of Silent Love* by A Carthusian (London: Darton, Longman & Todd, 1993), and my 'Apophatic prayer as a theological model' in *Literature and Theology* (December 1993), pp. 325–53.

16 For an extended practical exposition, see the series by Carthusian writers cited above. See also O. Clément, *The Roots of Christian*

Mysticism (London: New City, 1993), and André Louf, *Turning Into Grace* (London: Darton, Longman & Todd, 1993).

17 Benedicta Ward, *Harlots of the Desert* (London: Mowbray, 1987).

18 It is interesting that the REB has far and away the most sensual of all the translations of this passage.

19 See Marvin Shaw, *The Paradox of Intention* (Atlanta: Scholars Press, 1988).

20 The full text of this section had to be cut, due to length. It is available on request from the author.

21 A perennial problem, it is acknowledged in Benedict's *Rule*, ch. 62. There has begun a movement in men's communities whereby the superior can be a layperson, but clericalism still predominates.

22 '. . . the women were virtual prisoners, living in a state of permanent squabbling and bickering, largely induced by insecurity. The only security they had was their husband's favor': Jung Chang on the competitive envy of concubines in *Wild Swans* (London: HarperCollins, 1993), p. 40. For 'husband' read 'male clergy'.

23 For example, on a rare occasion when I agreed to facilitate a workshop for about forty mostly middle-aged women, there were two clergymen present, an Anglican in a collar and a Nonconformist in civvies, and a newly ordained Anglican woman deacon, also in a collar. As the day progressed, the misery and pain these women had experienced at the hands of clergy started to pour out, obviously the first time they had ever dared to speak. I asked the clergy present, particularly the woman deacon, if they wanted to respond. The men participated in a low-key, penitential way; the woman deacon declined. In the afternoon we returned to a more conventional format. Afterwards, the men were very happy with the way the day had gone; the woman deacon vanished. A week later I was informed that she had written to the bishop, the suffragan, and virtually every diocesan official who might remotely be connected with education, complaining, in effect, that I was not in lockstep with the clergy and the official party line.

The terrible pain of exclusion and condemnation among the general public is more widespread than the clergy may wish to admit, and certainly more than they want to know. At the last Affirming Catholicism meeting I ever attended—it had gradually been taken over by the clergy, who were all sitting on one side of the table, while the four laypeople (both men and women) sat on the other—I simply lost it. I was also terrified, and so didn't articulate very well. When my outpouring had ended, the clergy hastily turned to another laywoman there, who turned out to be the omsbudsperson for the diocese, saying surely my perception wasn't representative. Sitting there in her plaid skirt, white blouse and sweater, she had the guts to say quietly 'I'm afraid that's exactly the way it is'.

24 Not only psychologically, sexually and socially abusive: there is the shocking fact that the inventor of the neutron bomb is an Anglican (ECUSA) priest.

25 'Girard's work has been devoted to analysing these cycles of violence which emerge because we only desire that which another person finds desirable. Our acts of imitation, therefore, generate conflict. This mimetic conflict reaches a point where a victim is found who can act as a scapegoat. The scapegoat then unites the warring factions and creates a synthetic panacea which, in its turn, is deemed to be sacred. Girard develops his ideas on the scapegoat mechanism in his books *Violence and the Sacred* (1972, tr. 1977) and *The Scapegoat* (1982, tr. 1987). In his book *Things Hidden Since the Foundation of the World* (1978), Girard examines how Christ effectively absorbs and defeats the scapegoat mechanism and the cycles of violence it both pacifies and perpetuates'— Graham Ward.

26 The wordless gestures of the Fraction rite sum up the entire liturgy, providing a potentially fathomless resource for meditation and for study for liturgical renewal. It sends the message that there is no union without sacrifice, no unity except through our acknowledged brokenness, for pain and otherness is what humans have most in common. ECUSA's prayer book has possibly the best extant Fraction rite, surrounded by silence. The Host is held up and broken, the two halves held widely apart for all to see, the words 'Christ our Passover is sacrificed for us' are spoken, to which the response is 'Therefore let us keep the feast'. This liturgical introduction in the 1979 Prayer Book won immediate and virtually universal acceptance.

27 Cf. Anthony Bloom in *Courage to Pray* (London: Darton, Longman & Todd, 1973).

28 Because sacred signs efface themselves, clumsy and theologically questionable inclusive language is often more opaque, more of a barrier to God than a help, because it refocuses the attention of the worshippers on themselves. While it is salutary to get rid of phrases such as 'us men' and 'all men' and language about abhorring wombs, to say in the context of the Eucharist 'our brother Jesus' as opposed to 'our Lord Jesus Christ' (to cite only one example) is mistaken, in part because our focus is on the historical *Christ*, not on the historical Jesus (the 'humanity of Christ' is only peripherally related to the historical Jesus). See Elizabeth A. Johnson, *She Who Is* (New York: Crossroad, 1993), p. 73. Such language also misses the point that the word 'Lord' is

not about hierarchy but a signifier for transcendence. More profoundly, such a change destroys the paradoxes necessary to contemplative prayer, i.e., the Lord who becomes a servant; the God who becomes a human being; divinity that is epitomized in lowliness; and, if one requires a feminist twist, the paradox of a prodigally generous, self-outpouring, selfless God indicated by a male signifier. Further, to change 'Bridegroom' to 'friend' (e.g., in the Advent hymn 'Wachet auf') obliterates the use and transfiguration of eros which is essential to prayer. There are very good psychospiritual reasons that mystical language is often profoundly erotic; prayer involves the entire being and eros or 'sexuality' is the animator of intention. See V. Gillespie and M. Ross, 'The apophatic image: the poetics of effacement in Julian of Norwich' in *The Medieval Mystical Tradition in England*, vol. V, ed. Marion Glasscoe (Cambridge: D. S. Brewer), and my 'Sexuality, otherness and the truth of the self', *Vox Benedictina* (Winter 1993) and 'Apophatic prayer as a theological model', cited above.

29 See Paul Bradshaw, *Liturgical Presidency in the Early Church* (Grove Books, 1983), also quoted in my *Pillars of Flame: Power, Priesthood and Spiritual Maturity* (London: SCM, 1988), p. 35.

30 *Pillars*, p. 24.

31 Of many such declarations, see the Oxford University Sermon by Graham Ward (7 November 1993): '. . . It is not sufficient for theology to go on pretending that the culture and society we live in is the same as Matthew Arnold's. It isn't. Theology can no longer continue using . . . tools it honed for its use in modernity . . . a series of correlations between God and the world. Apologetics can only function on the assumption of shared values between theology, culture and society. But postmodernity is the recognition that there are no shared values, no common roots. Meaning is not shared, it is constructed and contingent. So the study of theology, if it is ever going to speak and resonate again in contemporary society, has to change; and change radically . . . its increasing irrelevance is in fact part of the reason for its decline among colleges in this University.'

32 See *The Paradox of Intention* and the works on apophasis cited above.

33 See Bruce Gregory, *Inventing Reality: Physics as Language* (New York: Wiley, 1990).

34 A three-month internship spent in a hospital where as much or more is learnt by ordinands about themselves as how to meet the spiritual needs of the sick and dying.

35 See my 'Sexuality, otherness and the truth of the self', cited above.

36 See Sister Lavinia Byrne's description of 'spiritual direction' as a

'master–slave' relationship in *Sharing the Vision* (London: SPCK, 1989), p. 21.

37 'The West has become a haven for spiritual charlatans': Sogyal Rinpoche in *The Tibetan Book of Living and Dying* (HarperSanFrancisco, 1992), an invaluable book for getting fresh perspective.

    This is not, however, to idealize Tibetan Buddhism, which shares many of the same problems with Christianity and other religions. It is only recently, for example, that the Dalai Lama has encouraged Tibetan nuns to become literate and read the scriptures (he is the first to do so) or to note the squalor and poverty in which they often live.

38 For an apt parable, see Julian Barnes's comments on the decline of caroling in 'Letter from London: the Maggie years', *The New Yorker* (15 November 1993).

39 *The Way of Silent Love*, vol. III, forthcoming.

40 'I use the term "call" not in the sense of a datable experience, but as a sense that one's life has a theonomous cast, is deeply referred to the purposes of God, which gives freedom and distance and perspective in relation to all other concerns. Such a call is not an event, but an ongoing dynamic of a growing and powerful claim [on the one being called] ... We need to recognize that such a sense of call in our time is profoundly countercultural, because the primary ideological voices of our time are the voices of autonomy: to do one's own thing, self-actualization, self-assertion, self-fulfillment. The ideology of our time is to propose that one can live "an uncalled life," one not referred to any purpose beyond one's self ... If the ideology of autonomy talks us out of our call as it talked Ancient Israel out of its call, we too may settle for idolatries that feel and sound like a call. An idolatrous alternative may take the form of a moral crusade in which we focus on one moral issue to the neglect of everything else ... a dogmatic crusade, which is often a disguised form of maintaining monopoly, an ecclesiastical passion, or an echo of civil religion ... all diversionary activities to keep from facing the yielding in obedience that belongs to all who are called by this God... They are in fact attempts to keep the known world safe, to preclude the dismantling work of Yahweh... Jeremiah understands call to be deeper and more dangerous. The holy purposes of God move in upon and against all of our arrangements... [Jeremiah's] yearning for God is not a pious or mystical quest. It is a court of last resort after every other yearning has failed (18:19)': Brueggemann, pp. 18–22.

41 See Penelope Jamieson, 'The shadow of God: issues of vocation

for women' (The Orr Memorial Lecture, 1993; Huron College, London, Ontario).

42 'Power is a fabrication, a fraud that separates men from their humanity': Stephen Schiff, commenting on the work of Alan Bennett, *The New Yorker* (6 September 1993). The Native American writer Gerald Vizenor, in his story 'The Moccasin Game', has the same insight: 'Men who had dreamed too much [i.e., their own projections instead of waiting for a complete vision] were transformed with only parts of birds and animals ... Migizi, the eagle, was no more than the head of the bald eagle and he screeched his words.

' "Migizi pretends to be human because he tried so hard to be an eagle," said Nawina. "He shouts that the men who dream too much, the men who try so hard to escape their human bodies, are the men with weak visions. The humans with unbroken visions hold the bear and eagle in their hearts. Baapi and the hand talkers [deaf-mutes] are the ones with visions, and they do not wear feathers and claws as a disguise" ': *Earth Song, Sky Spirit*, ed. Clifford E. Trafzer (Anchor, 1992).

43 *The Way of Silent Love*, vol. III, forthcoming, cited above.

44 'Whenever someone still unconditionally hopes beyond all empirical hopelessness; wherever a particular joy is experienced as the promise of a joy that is limitless; wherever a person loves with unconditional faithfulness and resolve, although the frailty of such love on both sides cannot possibly legitimize this unconditional determination; wherever radical responsibility towards a moral obligation is maintained, even when it seemingly leads only to disaster; wherever the relentlessness of truth is experienced and unconditionally accepted and grasped; wherever the unsurmountable discrepancy between what is individual and what is social in the plurality of man's different destinies is endured in a seemingly unjustified resolve to hope for the meaning and blessedness which reconciles everything ... in all these situations God ... is already experienced and accepted, even if this is not expressly and objectively formulated'; Karl Rahner SJ, 'Religious feeling inside and outside the Church' in *Theological Investigations*, vol. 17 (New York: Crossroad, 1981), pp. 236–37.

45 See my *Seasons of Death and Life* (San Francisco: HarperSanFrancisco, 1990).

46 Isaiah 40.31.

Bibliography

Julian Barnes, 'Letter from London: the Maggie years', *The New Yorker* 82–89 (15 November 1993).

Anthony Bloom, *Courage to Pray* (London: Darton, Longman & Todd, 1973).

Paul Bradshaw, *Liturgical Presidency in the Early Church* (Nottingham: Grove Books, 1983).

Walter Brueggemann, *Hopeful Imagination* (London: SCM, 1992).

Lavinia Byrne, *Sharing the Vision* (London: SPCK, 1989).

A Carthusian, *The Way of Silent Love* (London: Darton, Longman & Todd, 1993).

A Carthusian, *The Way of Silent Love*, vol. III (London: Darton, Longman & Todd, forthcoming).

Jung Chang, *Wild Swans* (London: HarperCollins, 1993).

O. Clément, *The Roots of Christian Mysticism* (London: New City, 1993).

V. Gillespie and M. Ross, 'The apophatic image: the poetics of effacement in Julian of Norwich' in *The Medieval Mystical Tradition in England*, vol. V, ed. Marion Glasscoe (Cambridge: D. S. Brewer, 1992).

René Girard, *Violence and the Sacred* (Baltimore: Johns Hopkins, 1972 (tr. 1977)).

The Scapegoat (Baltimore: Johns Hopkins, 1982 (tr. 1987)).

Things Hidden Since the Foundation of the World (London: The Athlone Press, 1978).

Bruce Gregory, *Inventing Reality: Physics as Language* (New York: Wiley, 1990).

Aloys Grillmeier SJ, tr. John Bowden, *Christ in Christian Tradition*, vol. I (London: Mowbray, 1975).

Penelope Jamieson, 'The shadow of God: issues of vocation for women' (The Orr Memorial Lecture; London, Ontario: Huron College, 1993).

Elizabeth A. Johnson, *She Who Is* (New York: Crossroad, 1993).

Ursula Le Guin, *The Farthest Shore* (New York: Bantam, 1969).

André Louf, *Tuning Into Grace* (London: Darton, Longman & Todd, 1993).

Justin McCann (tr.), *The Rule of St Benedict* (London: Sheed and Ward, 1976).

W. McKane, *Proverbs* (London: SCM, 1981).

Karl Rahner SJ, 'Religious feeling inside and outside the Church' in *Theological Investigations*, vol. 17 (New York: Crossroad, 1981), pp. 236–37.

Sogyal Rinpoche, *The Tibetan Book of Living and Dying* (San Francisco: HarperSanFrancisco, 1992).

Maggie Ross, *The Fountain and the Furnace* (Mahwah: Paulist, 1987).

Pillars of Flame: Power, Priesthood and Spiritual Maturity (London: SCM, 1988).

Seasons of Death and Life (San Francisco: HarperSanFrancisco, 1990).

The Fire of Your Life (London: Darton, Longman & Todd, 1992).

'Apophatic prayer as a theological model: seeking coordinates in the ineffable', *Literature and Theology* (December 1993), pp. 325–53.

'Sexuality, otherness and the truth of the self', *Vox Benedictina* (Winter 1993).

Stephen Schiff, 'The poet of embarrassment', *The New Yorker* (6 September 1993), pp. 92–101.

Margaret O'Brien Steinfels, 'The laity and the leadership crisis', *Commonweal* 8 (10 September 1993), 16–2.

Stephen Sykes, 'Vision and voting: reflections on the Anglican doctrine of the Church' in *Living the Mystery* (London: Darton, Longman & Todd, 1994).

Clifford E. Trafzer (ed.), *Earth Song, Sky Spirit* (New York: Anchor, 1992).

Hans Urs von Balthasar, *The Glory of the Lord*, vol. I (Edinburgh: T. & T. Clark, 1982).

Benedicta Ward, *Harlots of the Desert* (London: Mowbray, 1987).

8

Living a mystery: a Roman Catholic perspective

JACKIE HAWKINS

When the idea of priesthood first came into my mind fourteen years ago, putting it into speech felt like mouthing an obscenity. I remember walking with a Jesuit friend for a whole afternoon in the hills round St Beuno's in North Wales trying to make this simple statement to him. He had been my retreat director a few weeks before and was shortly to return to Africa. I never did manage it. It still isn't easy. This extreme sense of taboo may seem extraordinary today but although the debate about women priests was well under way in the Church of England at that time, it was not being aired in the public arena and I did not have any ecumenical experience to make me aware of it. My own faith had only recently started to stir into something like adult maturity and I was not much involved in any 'thinking' church groups or networks. The word 'feminism' had yet to enter my vocabulary, let alone my consciousness!

Why did this idea come to me in a Church where the idea of priesthood and, indeed, all formal leadership, authority, power, responsibility and decision-making has the narrowest of models—that of the ordained, celibate male? How could I as a Roman Catholic laywoman belong in the Church as a priest? For many years I was living a mystery. These many years later I can articulate an explanation. As a woman and as a priest I did not belong in *that* Church but in a future one, the Church conceived in the reforms of the Second Vatican Council but as yet unrealized. Largely unacknowledged in this country, but evolving at an ever-increasing pace, there is a dynamic, reformed and renewed

Roman Catholic Church in which ordained ministry will be open to me, or women like me, on the same terms as men. This will be a reformed priesthood, which I prefer to call ordained ministry, which will be part of such wide-ranging reform that the Church as it was in the 1960s and before the Council will be unrecognizable.

My experience is that the problem of clericalism in Christian leadership is widely acknowledged across the mainstream denominations, although it is perhaps most obvious in the Roman Catholic Church where it is being forced to a visible crisis, largely because of mandatory celibacy and all that that is now seen to stand for. But it is a general challenge, and I therefore write my comments on the assumption that ordained Christian leadership remains in need of radical reform in all the mainstream Churches despite the welcome new presence of women priests in the Church of England.

The new presence of women priests in our sister Church is not in fact the challenge to the Roman Catholic Church that many people suppose it is, despite rumblings from Rome. For many Roman Catholics who have given serious consideration to the ordination of women it is a matter that is taken for granted as proper to the full theological understanding of women's role in the Christian Church, as well as being a serious matter of justice. The real challenge comes from within, rooted in the theology of the Second Vatican Council and the post-conciliar developments which have followed. At the Council, the understanding that the presence and action of the Holy Spirit is present throughout the whole people of God through baptism was rediscovered and restated, and this, as it is being experienced as the truth, is undermining the traditional clerical power-base of the Roman Catholic Church. The shift is not towards the empowerment of women as priests, but to the proper empowerment of all baptized believers among whom ordained leaders, both men and women, will serve, exercising an appropriate, not monopolistic, authority.

I would also like to dispel the common misconception that religious sisters are frustrated priests, having settled for the nearest substitute to priesthood. Nor are they comfortable with the superior spirituality so often attributed to them by laypeople.

Roman Catholic religious sisters are in fact laypeople. Some religious sisters do feel that priesthood as well as community life is their calling. Most do not. Some are denied the exercise of their Order's charism by our monopolistic clerical powers. Dominican sisters, for example, members of the Order of Preachers, may not preach in the ordinary course of the Catholic Church's worship; only the ordained may preach the homily immediately after the gospel. This practice is sometimes set aside, but only a minority of Catholics in this country have ever seen a woman preach at Mass. (Ironically, this includes the priests-in-formation in at least one major seminary in England where the few full-time women staff members are encouraged to preach at Mass. When priests, these same men are bound to ensure that women do not preach at their Masses.) Vocationally, lay women are in much the same position. Increasing numbers want to exercise full responsible Christian adulthood but only a few feel called to be an ordained minister. None that I know wish to be ordained into the present system. Instead they spend their time and commitment on helping others to come to an understanding of their baptismal mission, their priority being a reformed Catholic Church rather than their own vocation. However, a number of younger Roman Catholic women have, I understand, chosen to train for Anglican orders.

Nevertheless, the Roman Catholic Church in this country owes a great deal to the Church of England for bringing the issue of women's ordination firmly into our consciousness with the thorough and high-quality debate offered in the public media in the past few years, and through the presence of ordained women as deacons and now priests in our local communities and ecumenical experiences. It has also progressed considerably the Roman Catholic debate on ministry by provoking discussion in which different parties within the Church have come to realize their common ground.

If part of the purpose of this book is to look at the difference that ordained women will make to the Church then it will by now be obvious that my reflections arise from a very different context from that of Church of England commentators. Having been a member of MOW for a decade or so I am, however, familiar with what has been happening in the Church of England in recent years. As I see it, Anglican women are commenting on how they will affect the model of Church which has been their experience for some years, and which remains and will continue to remain for the foreseeable future. Theirs is a specific, identifiable framework within which to operate in the here and now. A Roman Catholic Church which will ordain women is essentially a vision for the medium-term future. This, I think, is the crux of the difference between the way the Roman Catholic Church is coming to the question of the ordination of women and the way that it has happened in the Church of England. Given the models of authority and governance in the Church of England, ordination has become a realizable possibility for Anglican women within the present institutional structure. It had already been achieved by women in other parts of the Anglican communion, too. The course of events over the past eighteen months has determined that reform of clericalism, and therefore ministry, in the Church of England will happen with women working from within the system. In the Roman Catholic Church, widespread radical reform is preceding the ordination of women. It is the reform which will give rise to ordained women, rather than vice versa.

As I have briefly mentioned, the reform is not just about clericalism or priesthood, it is about the whole nature of the dynamic of the Church. The ordination of women will be one among many reforms. My story of needing a 'new Church' in which to be an ordained leader, and the anachronistic situation in which I find myself as a mature, adult Christian in a system which requires immature subordination to hierarchy and to God, are typical of the experience of thousands of Roman Catholics throughout the country, including many priests. One way or another, at different times and places, in fits and starts or slowly and steadily, people like me have absorbed the theology of Vatican II and undergone a form of conversion. It is a process which continues. All sorts of individuals and groups are beginning to grasp the real implications of the universal call to holiness and the mission of all the baptized, the fundamental statements of reform set out in the documents on *The Constitution of the Church* and *The Church in the Modern World* at the Second Vatican Council. There is a widening and deepening of our understanding of ministry and of the right relationship of people with God and with each other, and people caught up in this conversion process in the Roman Catholic Church are experiencing the truth of this. Above all, many women are discarding the Christian parameters laid down by the patriarchal system of centuries and instead are learning to define their own Christian identities out of their newly discovered self-knowledge and experience of God. This new, richer understanding of Christian identity and experience for both men and women will bring about widespread changes, one of which will be to have women in the ordained ministry.

My story of being called to Christian adulthood through the path to priesthood may appear to be the way that is most challenging to a system which claims divine institution for its male exclusivity. But the conclusions based on the reflections on my own experiences are not just my own. What I offer here are observations discussed and shared with many others: laywomen, including religious sisters, and men, lay, religious and ordained. Inevitably I must reflect, too, on the impact of the vast numbers of women who undertake extensive responsibilities within the Roman Catholic Church already, a fact often not appreciated by those outside the Roman Catholic Church. If there is a gender difference at work in Christian leadership, then the effect that women have must be being widely felt already. Although the concern of this book is with the experience and expression of these qualities in the visible leader of the faith community, i.e. the priest as the representative of Christ, ordained women in the Roman Catholic Church will only become a focus for these qualities long after they are well established within the Church as a whole. Ordination will be the culmination of the acceptance and acknowledgement of women's qualities, rather than their starting point.

*

Although baptized a Roman Catholic I came from a home of intense religious hostility and attended a Catholic school only from the age of eleven. My mother, a woman of great intelligence and formidable strengths, had a loathing for the Catholic Church only possible for an embittered convert of her personal strength. I was not allowed to attend any religious education lessons. Consequently, years later when Vatican II came along, I was largely free of the cradle Catholic's 'hang-ups' which haunt so many. I'm certain that the irony of this did not escape my mother in her later, but barely mellower years as my desire for some overtly 'religious' work became obvious. Back at school, despite my mother's efforts, I was eventually nobbled by a keen nun and became a rather desultory practising Catholic not untypical of the pre-Vatican II Church.

For various reasons I always had to be independent from a very early age; I tended not to join groups or to be only on the fringe. I do not 'buy into packages' as someone recently put it. This applied to the Church too, so I find that as an institution it has played a far less central role in my development of faith and my concept of God than for many other people. Nor do I have the sentimental feelings of nostalgia and loyalty so deeply ingrained in more traditional Catholics. This independence from the Church 'package', while marginalizing in many ways, has also been a strength in enabling me not to mistake the Church for God and to stay—just—within an institution which has a great deal wrong with it; and which, at the institutional level, is only able to pay lip service to the latter part of the statement that it is 'ever holy, and ever in need of reform' (*The Constitution of the Church*, Vatican II).

The mystery of priesthood has drifted in and out of my life. First it was about being a woman and a priest. Later, and more importantly, it became about the meaning of priesthood itself as I came to understand the powerful implication of the baptismal dynamic for every Christian. I have no doubt that the enforced waiting has led me to a more profound understanding of priesthood than if I had been able to be accepted, after appropriate selection, into the system as it stands. Not being able to buy into the present system gave me the opportunity to look long and deep. What was it that I felt called to that I named as priesthood? Was that what I saw in the present system? If so, why could I not be part of it? If not, how could the difference be articulated? Was I mistaken, or was the present model of priesthood flawed?

I have never doubted the truth of my call to priesthood

although for most of the fourteen years until now it has only
been part of my conscious life from time to time. The first time
I spoke of it was one summer at the beginning of the 1980s
when I was on holiday in the West Country. I was in Exeter for
the day while my car was being repaired. In the early morning
peace of the beautiful cathedral I screwed up my courage and
decided to try out my thoughts on an open-minded, progressive
member of the Chapter—if there was one. A steward suggested
the Treasurer, Canon Mawson. Feeling extremely nervous I
finally made myself ring his bell. He was very welcoming. He
said he had been visited the previous day by a woman preparing
for ordination in New Zealand, and he was the first of many
Anglicans over the years to say that, because of our relative
authority systems, Rome would probably beat the Church of
England to it in ordaining women. He gave me an image I have
always found helpful: 'See it as a cross-country journey', he said,
'where you can only see one stile at a time.' It's proving one hell
of a journey!

Life was extremely tough at the time. I was bringing up my
sons on my own in difficult circumstances which were not obvious to outsiders. I was fortunate that my faith deepened in that
time. Through a combination of occasional lectures on Vatican
II given by a quietly radical priest, meeting a few like-minded
people, and through parish ministry of various sorts, my understanding grew too. I came across Ignatian spirituality, totally
suited to my nature, and this proved my life-line when conserva-
tism gripped my parish in the form of a new parish priest. As a
questioning Catholic woman with a strong personality I was to
be actively discouraged, despite my proven abilities. Priesthood
surfaced again in my mind. If I was not allowed to express my
response to God by using my gifts as a lay person, what chance
had my gifts as a priest? I was also increasingly scandalized at
what I saw as the travesty of Jesus' leadership as modelled by
the Roman Catholic Church. I took my frustration, confusion
and unhappiness to a Jesuit acquaintance. He suggested that I
look at my priesthood within the Ignatian Exercises. I agreed—
without knowing what on earth that meant. I tend to fall into
things like this. I had done a couple of eight-day retreats and
liked the style. With a brilliant director I undertook the Exercises

by the Nineteenth Annotation in just a few months. The crux of the experience was as follows.

A decade before, I had been expecting a third child. She had died when I was seven months pregnant and the birth had to be induced. Bereavement in these circumstances was not dealt with as sensitively then as it is now. Such a death was not regarded as that of a real person. But for me, and my husband, we had lost a real person, someone we loved already as one of our family. A life had been extinguished which had been a very present reality. One day during the Exercises, I wept as I had only ever wept over the death of this child and the loss of my marriage. I knew that God had stripped my priesthood from me. The experience was synonymous with the understanding that came through the symbol of my dead baby. Just as that child had come to life and had her reality within me but was hidden from the world, so my priesthood had been conceived and grown within me, a vivid and mysterious reality, but for which there was no visible evidence in the world beyond me. As with my daughter, that which I grieved for was not real to anyone other than myself. At the time I did not realize how crucial was my acceptance of this stripping away. Some weeks later, before the Exercises ended, my calling was restored to me, gently but with great power.

Priesthood then went underground while the more general sense of being drawn to some overtly religious work made itself felt. During the years of family life I had decided that I would have to retrain for a new career, as the world of consumer marketing in which I had previously worked had long ceased to be attractive. I combined meeting the challenge of bringing up my teenage sons with a wide variety of voluntary work, work which gave me invaluable insights into myself and my abilities. Part of this was as a journalist for local radio religious broadcasting. Starting just before the station went on air, I spent five years in this ecumenical work, representing the life of as many Christian communities in the catchment area as wanted to co-operate. I did it because I had long felt strongly that the Church is ineffective in using the broadcast media. It was richly rewarding as I was drawn into the lives of so many communities. I learnt their stories and beliefs, their strengths and weaknesses, and I gave and received friendship. Most significantly of all in this present context, after two or three years, people began to ask if I felt 'called to ministry' or 'called to preach', using whatever was the terminology of their denomination for formal Christian leadership. A number of Christian communities, quite independently, were acknowledging my qualities and my calling as a Christian leader.

At one stage I had told a Roman Catholic canon of what I believed to be my vocation. I did that because he moved widely in church circles and I wanted to ensure that he could never say, in any discussion about the ordination of women, that he didn't know any woman who wanted it. He triumphantly pointed out that priestly vocation is not simply a personal thing but a call by the community. He was, of course, quite right, as I later understood more fully. What was so objectionable in his attitude was his dishonesty about the present form of being 'called by the community' in the Roman Catholic Church which is actually a process stylized out of all recognition, wholly in the hands of the bishop and a few of his advisers. Furthermore, Roman Catholic communities as such have no expectation of recognizing anyone as a priest/leader in the sense that this might carry any weight, and certainly not a woman, who is excluded by her sex from all formal leadership. Any woman who is distinctive enough to show what might be called vigorous leadership qualities is almost certainly labelled a trouble-maker, maverick or a crank. Only by exercising my leadership qualities as a Roman Catholic in an area in which the Church is largely uninterested, broadcasting—and the clergy therefore unthreatened—and under the ecumenical gaze, was I able to receive the affirmation of Christians who thought of leadership more widely than as simply belonging to celibate men.

As my children approached the time when they would leave home to study I decided that I needed some formal theological education. This would give me some credibility in the eyes of those I assumed to be my future employers, the Catholic bishops. I describe my time at Heythrop as putting theological flesh on the bones of my faith experience. I acquired the evidence to support what my instincts had been telling me about faith and Church over the preceding few years. But two other things happened. Lay employment had been expanding significantly in the eighties. Almost as soon as I stepped over Heythrop's threshold this trend started to collapse, for an assortment of reasons, and a notable conservative retrenchment set in. Secondly, my combination of knowledge and experience led me to understand the Church as something so different from the current institutional model that I knew I could never work with integrity as its representative. I had arrived, for reasons unrelated to my personal call to priesthood, at the understanding of the need for a new church. Far from my route becoming clearer, it became further confused.

The insights that I can now articulate about my call to ordained ministry are made up of the accumulation of fourteen years of experience, intuition and knowledge that have come together in an understanding which continues to deepen. This enforced fast from priestly ministry, so to speak, has sharpened my awareness of what it is about. The waiting and 'pondering these things in my heart' has, I believe, given me a much deeper understanding of what priesthood is than many of the men who are able to go straight into the system of priestly formation. This is not necessarily a criticism—if a system is there and you are eligible, why look further than you need? Where I and other women in waiting find common ground is among priests who have been ordained for a number of years and are increasingly uncomfortable with the model of priesthood in which they were formed and which remains the institutional model, still used in seminary training with the odd cosmetic change. They are unhappy with their monopoly of institutional power, however effectively they delegate, recognizing that participation in Christian mission is the baptismal right of all believers, not something to be delegated as a favour to them by the priest.

The wider reforms to which I have referred, rooted in the growing understanding of the equality of baptism, are rapidly changing Roman Catholics' perception and expectation of who may be gifted with leadership qualities. As well as in Roman Catholic schools, in which religious sisters have an established historical role, gifted women now hold a significant number of leading roles in the very public spheres of justice and peace work, religious education and aid organizations. In more limited circles, women are leaders in the world of spirituality and theology, both practical and academic, and in pastoral work of all sorts, and perhaps above all in parish ministries and catechetics. This exercise of their gifts given by the Spirit to women is familiarizing people with women who have 'put on Christ' in their baptism and are wanting to express this fully in their lives. Whether or not they would immediately put the tag 'leader' on all of these women, there is no doubt that Roman Catholics in this country, by and large, are increasingly familiar with women leaders as part of normal parish life.

The number of women, religious and lay, working in the field of spirituality, especially in spiritual direction and retreat giving, places women firmly at the core of Christian faith life in the role of spiritual guide, formerly regarded as almost solely the role of the priest (at least in the last couple of centuries). The evident quality and gifts of these women raises the question for many people as to why women should not be priests, and the spiritual leaders of Christian communities? In a sense it is but a short step to seeing women as spiritual leaders of the community in this way, when there is so much visible, dynamic witnessing to Christ already self-evidently in progress. The required paradigm shift may seem to demand a huge leap, but I believe for Roman Catholics genuinely seeking an effective Church for the future, the process of conversion towards accepting women as ordained leaders is well under way.

My present career illustrates how Roman Catholic women are also being recognized more widely as authentic leaders. This, I must say, is due in no small measure to the appointment three years ago or so of Sister Lavinia Byrne IBVM to a senior executive post in the Council of Churches for Britain and Ireland, becoming in the process that rarity, a Roman Catholic woman with public authority. The effect on raising the public profile of able Roman Catholic women has been remarkable as she has networked with others to meet the impossible demands on her personal time. At present I am executive editor of two highly regarded international spirituality journals. This is a far cry from the parish community—or its future equivalent—where I would like to minister to people in the name of Christ in the nitty-gritty of their ordinary lives. But it has opened significant doors. It is another symptom of how so many factors are working together to create the new Church which will accept ordained women. Speakers are needed for the many theology and study courses which are run regularly, especially in Lent, and ecumenically since the national initiative of Lent '86. Organizers now look beyond Roman Catholic clergy for a view from that denomination. Some even recognize that there is a significant number of lay people, especially women, who are better informed than many of the clergy. In short, they are accepted as providing as valid a view of the Roman Catholic scene as a priest. In this way, Roman Catholics attending these courses or study days themselves become accustomed to seeing and hearing Catholic women speak authoritatively. This is a very helpful development for me, as speaking in this way is something I do well and to which I find people respond. Best of all it has led to invitations to preach, a gift I am denied by law to exercise in my own Church.

It is not my purpose to give an exhaustive list of the qualities of women and how they will bear on priesthood. Such qualities have been described at length in the writings of women working in all aspects of Christian activity. But I will identify a few qualities which I think will be especially significant to the Roman Catholic Church in the wake of the aggressively male, patriarchal system which is our present experience. There is, for instance, the attitude to institution. For certain sections of the Roman Catholic Church the centralized (if not monarchical), authoritarian institution of the past 150 years seems to have become an end in itself, despite the briefly hopeful rediscovery of collegiality during Vatican II. In a rigid form of institution, conformers are rewarded, the institution counts for more than its members and not to conform puts at risk all that the institution provides, especially for its officials—power, status, security, identity. Far more than in any other denomination, most Catholic priests have their identity locked into the institution. Although I mentioned earlier my personal reasons for not being institutionally inclined, it is recognized that women in general do not take on institutional packages as blindly as many men: they are not so prepared to defend the flawed, or the indefensible, for the sake of a false sense of unity. Perhaps this is because for most of history women have not been a part of institutional life in any way that was to their real advantage. They have had nothing to gain by pretending that an institution is any better than it really is, nor anything to lose by being honest about its flaws.

Vatican II rediscovered the dynamic of the Church in the world, and dynamism is incompatible with rigidity and authoritarianism. The Church needs to become again a much more loosely-knit, flexible organization to accommodate the gospel dynamic. Rather than trying to distort human nature in order to live by some rigid set of rules, it needs to become a Church much more akin to the informal community groups in which women have traditionally nurtured, reconciled and worked with individual strengths and weaknesses to achieve wide-reaching benefits, both collective and individual. There is, of course, an unavoidable tension in an ongoing institution needing some form of order which is flexible enough to embrace change yet cohesive enough to provide a sense of stability. Flexibility will apply to priesthood too; once it no longer monopolizes ministry there is no reason why it should be full time, permanent, or life long. And women have age-long experience of changing life direction several times over, if only through biological dictates.

Vatican II views all baptized believers as in a continuing process of maturing. Women, I believe, find this interpretation congenial for they more naturally want to move members of their believing community into a state of mutual, mature interdependence of faith, rather than maintain the hierarchical ranks of states of holiness which is the mindset of centuries. Sensing that the accusation of stereotype is never far away, I nevertheless wish to suggest from my own experience as a wife and mother that women have a particular awareness of the need to bring each individual within their care to 'fullness of being'. (I of course acknowledge other contexts in which nurturing is practised but I cannot speak for them as specifically.)

This nurturing of children is about preparing individuals for healthy freedom and autonomy, letting the individual go so that he or she may learn to relate in a context of growing adulthood within mature interdependence. However imperfectly women carry out this task of nurturing and letting go, as mothers they encounter this fact of life—the formation of individual beings who need to shift from dependence to interdependence. While consistently preaching maturity in terms of the primacy of conscience, Roman Catholic authorities nevertheless continue to maintain in practice an authoritarian and patriarchal system of dependence.

So long as there are women priests who have experienced the 'old Church' with its seductive but utterly confining expectation/ definition of the woman's role, they will be alert to the need to nurture to the full the giftedness of each believer. Only through this awareness can real maturity be discovered, through exercising the freedom born of the Gospel. This will in turn enable each believer to become most fully what God has created her or him to be, however unlikely or uncomfortable that may seem to the institution. We will then be released to act as though we truly believe that the Spirit may blow where it will, that it is to be trusted; to know that it is creative beyond our wildest imaginings, and to rejoice in the way that all of this would revitalize Christian communities and their effect on the world.

Parental nurturing also contains the challenge of acknowledging weaknesses within the context of love. This is, of course, fundamental to Christianity; we are a Church of sinners. The Sacrament of Reconciliation currently has an uncertain role, if any, in the lives of many Catholics. It has been revamped in such a way that it is, potentially, a deeply moving encounter with God, but many priests lack the qualities or personal development which go with such a tender process. A priest recently mentioned to me in passionate terms how he believes that women will transform the Sacrament of Reconciliation. It was good to have his endorsement that women are less juridical and law-bound, and more ready to kneel before God with the sinner as one who is also frail and weak. The reformed rite of this sacrament is much more nuanced to looking gently but deeply at our weakness in the light of the gospel love of God, and seeking to nurture our goodness within that love rather than to condemn our failings. This is certainly the way many women would understand positive nurturing within a family, for both children and adults, even if they often fail.

Preaching, language, communication—women exercise all these very differently from men. A recent letter from a papal nuncio to a large gathering of clergy was more an exhortation along the lines of a bad general to his troops before battle than to colleagues, let alone brothers and fellow believers in Christ. Because all Roman Catholic official communications come from men (and one has no reason to think that the writers are other than men), the involvement of women, whether in the written or spoken word, would make a significant difference. This may well be put to the test in England and Wales with the unique appointment of a woman, Pat Jones, as Assistant General Secretary to the Bishops' Conference of England and Wales. Perceptible signs of her influence are watched for with interest.

Women speak more naturally out of their own experience. Men may use personal stories, but they often shift back to a rather cerebral, clinical way of developing the point. Men have, I believe, much more invested in their status, and in the image of their role, and they are more bound by history and expectation. As things stand, they have a good deal to lose. Prophetic women are, I believe, less interested in living up to an image rather than being themselves. And Roman Catholic women come to priesthood with personal knowledge of the harm done to self and others by priests who have regarded themselves as separate, apart, superior. The Catholic system is littered with clerical casualties. In being more openly self-revealing, women encourage others in the struggle with their weakness by sharing their own. This openness to the need for grace naturally leads to the ability to share something of the experiences of redemption and resurrection. In this way women may facilitate a real capacity within a community to reflect openly on the presence of God among its members, and a real capacity to build up the Body of Christ. This is already done very effectively, but on a short-term basis, in the RCIA (Rite of Christian Initiation of Adults) groups—courses of reflection and preparation for people interested in joining the Roman Catholic Church, but also used by people who are already Catholics. Most RCIA catechists are women. This role for a woman priest would therefore be familiar to many who are now Catholics but who associate it with a specific and occasional educating and formation process rather than with the normal course of parish life.

The ability and desire to take on and live out the vision of Church which was proposed by Vatican II is a matter of conversion, involving opportunity, openness of heart and the

action of the Holy Spirit. Many are way ahead of me in understanding, many are well behind. It is always a mystery as to why
opportunities are greater for some than for others. Reason and
facts have little to do with it. You cannot force conversion.

The situation was summed up for me in an unexpected experience in the summer of 1992 at one of the final MOW rallies
before the Synod vote that November. The summer session of
the Synod was meeting at York University in July. The entrance
of the main hall looked out across a small lake where a walkway
connected the two sides. As Synod representatives assembled for
the evening session, MOW members gathered on the other side
of this lake in vigil. The light was fading early in a grey evening
as we gently sang Taizé chants and lit our candles. People looked
across at us, their faces too far away to be seen clearly. I wondered
what they were thinking. Supporters came down the walkway to
happy, grateful greetings. As I looked across the water I felt a
profound sorrow as I glimpsed what it means to be so excluded,
misunderstood, shut out. The water between us became deeply
symbolic. Even if we could have walked across it, I felt that that
would not have been enough for some of the people on the other
side. And yet I did not blame them. The mystery, the struggle,
the puzzle of all that is meant by Christian truth hung in the
air and was embodied in us as women seeking priesthood.

For women in the Church of England, claiming their right to
priesthood was an issue sharply defined and now achieved. How
effectively they will reform ministry will be watched with great
interest. The process in the Roman Catholic Church is, I believe,
more evolutionary, with the ordination of women being the ultimate recognition of the qualities with which women are increasingly affecting the Church here and now. While it must be seen
as part of a larger movement of the Spirit, the importance of
this representation cannot be overestimated. The priest both
represents the believing community to God and represents Christ
to the community. Women will see themselves offered to God
more visibly in language, manner, sentiment, their whole way of
being, and what is in them of God will be reflected back more
authentically. In representing God through Christ, women will
model all that is feminine in God, affirming its goodness, representing the image in which women are made and for which they,

and others, should value them. This new imaging must surely influence the perception of male ordained ministry, but how this will come about is beyond the scope of my speculation.

As some aspects of priesthood, such as preaching and the leading of liturgy, open to me in non-Catholic contexts, I am still left living a mystery. Despite all that I believe to be true about developments in the Roman Catholic Church, I know nothing for certain about what may happen in my lifetime, however long that may prove to be. At the conclusion of a retreat of great importance to me in 1993, I meditated with Mary at the foot of the cross. At the end of it she said to me 'My son will honour you if you watch with him'. That's all I really know.

My thanks to Anne Brown, Judith Carpenter and Elizabeth Ridley for their comments in the preparation of this chapter.

9

Of priests and presidents

JANE SINCLAIR

The picture of a woman presiding at the eucharist has often been conjured up during the debates about the ordination of women to the priesthood in the Church of England. Icon of Christ, servant and shepherd, handmaid of the Lord, the head of the local church: these metaphors and many others have been bandied at women as images of horror to some, of renewal and hope to others. The fantasy of the woman priest seen only in sexual terms was given explicit voice by the former Bishop of London, the Right Reverend Graham Leonard, during the debates about priesthood in the mid-1980s. He could not help but see a woman priest at the altar as a creature to be embraced. Equally fantastic has been the vision of the woman priest as the image of the forgotten mother of the Church, nurturing all who come to her; or the vision of the woman priest as revolutionary sister paving the way for the overturning of all ecclesiastical and patriarchal institutions. The prospect of the ordination of women as priests and their visible presence at the centre of the action of the eucharist has acted as a focus of fearful and of hopeful expectation for many years.

Women are now ordained as priests and are becoming established as priests within the life of the Church, but the question remains an open one: what may realistically be expected to happen to the liturgical life of the Church as a result? What difference will the ordination of women as priests make on a Sunday morning in practice? Contrary to many of the fantasies which have emerged during the years of debate there will in

important respects be very little difference at all. To members
of church congregations who have enjoyed the liturgical ministry of women deacons, relatively little will change as their minister begins to exercise her priestly liturgical ministry. The same
order of service will be used, from the Alternative Service Book
or from the Book of Common Prayer. The same hymns and
songs will be sung. The same gestures will be used, with as
much or little variation as male priests have used according to
their height, size and brand of churchmanship. The same bread
and wine will be taken, the same thanks given, the same bread will
be broken and shared. The customary vesture used by those
presiding at the eucharist in a church will be worn, albeit in
some new designs if the church's own vestments cannot be made
to fit the new priest.

There will, however, be some differences; evident in different
ways to those who have experienced the ministry of women
deacons, and to those for whom the ministry of ordained
women is completely new. Women's voices will be heard speaking
or singing words which have, until now, been spoken or sung
liturgically only by men. Women will be seen to be presiding,
not simply assisting, at the eucharist, with all that that visible
liturgical presidency represents theologically and pastorally.
Women will be seen and heard to absolve and bless with the
priestly authority vested in them at their ordination. Men will
be seen as deacons, or co-ministers, to be assisting women who
are presiding at the eucharist. The perceptions and attitudes of
lay and ordained worshippers towards the liturgical and theological relationships of men and women will be challenged in ways
which may be quite unexpected.

All that is how worshippers may perceive and experience the
ministry of women priests as they begin to exercise their liturgical ministry of priesthood. And the danger is that that will be
that. Women priests and worshippers will acclimatize themselves
to the differences quite quickly. Those who do not experience
the regular ministry of a woman priest will take longer to acclimatize than those who do. Those who disagree fundamentally with
women priests run the danger of becoming increasingly divorced
from the regular liturgical life of the rest of the Church. The

women priests themselves will simply become as clericalized as their male counterparts.

Yet it need not, and ought not to be like that. One of the gifts which the protracted debate about the ordination of women has given to the Church of England is the gift of time to consider afresh theologies of priesthood, the nature of priestly ministry and how they are expressed liturgically. The question that faces the Church now is not so much 'how can women priests learn to be good presiders at the eucharist?', but 'how can the Church's self-understanding and mission be enriched by the diverse gifts and insights which female and male priests, deacons and lay people *together* bring to the celebration of its sacraments and the preaching of its Word?'

Some clearing of the theological and liturgical ground needs to happen first. The debates about the ordination of women have revealed some profound popular misconceptions of the role of the priest in the eucharist. To speak of the presiding priest at the eucharist as the 'icon of Christ' is often to assume that the eucharist is a re-enactment of the Last Supper, or of a post-resurrection meal with Jesus, with the priest representing the person of Christ to the congregation as Christ's disciples. The image is a powerful one, and easy to grasp. Yet no eucharist is a re-enactment of a meal with Jesus as such; it is a meal shared with and in Christ now, the Christ in whom the whole Christian community is baptized, Christ risen, ascended and glorified and now living among God's people. At the eucharist the presiding priest is as much a worshipper as any other member of the congregation. Certainly a priest has particular functions to fulfil in relation to the other members of the congregation. She or he functions as the president of the community in the ordering of its eucharistic worship, retelling the story of our redemption, praying aloud with and for the community, ensuring that the community is fed by Word and sacrament. But she or he only represents Christ in the community to the same degree as any other baptized Christian represents Christ to their community, contrary to the natural human inclination to put the priest on a holier pedestal than so-called ordinary Christians. We need to beware of reducing our eucharistic worship to the mere level of re-enactment Sunday by Sunday. It is much, much more than that.

The image of the woman priest at the eucharist as the nurturing mother figure of the church also needs to be challenged. Certainly the eucharist is about feeding and being fed, about growing together in Christ. And certainly images of nurture in the world at large are powerfully focused on the image of the nursing mother. Moreover, the feminine in biological terms has long been distorted or simply invisible in the Church's theology and liturgical practice. However, to project motherly and nurturing images onto priests because they are women is to deny those self-same qualities in male priests, and to narrow the eucharist down to being a meal primarily for comfort and growth. Such a theology is difficult to hold alongside the well-attested tradition recorded in I Corinthians 11 and in the gospels, that we are 'to do this in remembrance' of Jesus. The meal is about death and life, the coming of the Kingdom of God, the challenge to repentance, the call to bear witness in love and truth. Nurture and growth are part of that work, but are only a part.

Finally, the image of the priest as revolutionary sister working towards the overthrow of ecclesiastical and patriarchal institutions needs to be treated with care. Undoubtedly the advent of women as priests will effect change in the structures of the Church. With imagination and love, those changes it is to be hoped will be creative, bold and, in the best sense of the word, revolutionary. But in the context of the eucharist, itself a revolutionary meal, those changes are initially much more likely to be in the areas of perception and attitude than in radical new liturgies. Worshippers will see and hear new priests at work. Old assumptions about who priests are and what they do liturgically will be implicitly questioned, and actual practice is likely to be subtly altered. In part, the first generation of women priests is bound to mirror much of the present practice of the Church. There are few role models for the women to imitate, and acceptance in the Church at large demands a reasonable degree of conformity on the part of the new priests. Yet the work of this first generation of women ordained as priests will be vitally important in helping to shape the perceptions and practice of the women (and men) who follow them into ordained priestly ministry. For this reason it is important now for women ordained as priests not to create liturgical straitjackets into which others in turn will have to squeeze. Rather, there is an urgent need for the Church to seize the opportunities for liturgical formation afforded by the experience of its newest priests and to receive their creative liturgical insights and practice as gifts to be tested and developed.

*

The women who have been ordained during the first round of ordinations to the priesthood in 1994 bring some unique insights with them to priestly ministry and therefore to the liturgical ministry of the Church. The liturgical experience of women as deaconesses and deacons has led, during the 1970s and 1980s, in particular, to a wider prominence to the ministry of the deacon. Where a liturgical diaconal ministry functions, congregations have grown used to hearing a woman read the Gospel, preach, lead intercessions, prepare the gifts at the altar, stand by the presiding priest during the eucharistic prayer, distribute Communion, perform the ablutions and dismiss the assembly. Their traditional diaconal functions in the liturgy have become somewhat blurred by the experience of women having been appointed as deacons-in-charge of parishes. In these churches, women deacons have often functioned, *de facto*, as liturgical presidents, responsible for ordering all the worship in the church, with the exception of small but significant sections of the eucharist over which the visiting priest has presided. This experience has served to emphasize the strong link between pastoral care and liturgical presidency which exists within the life of the Church.

By contrast, other women deacons—many of whom are non-stipendiary—have been seen and heard to fulfil a distinctive liturgical role, but that role has in effect been simply that of an assistant to the priest, useful but not essential. To complicate the Church's self-understanding still further, the ordained male colleagues of women deacons have had scant opportunity to exercise their own diaconal liturgical ministry since the first year of their ordained ministry. The men preside as priests, and the women assist as deacons. The ordination of women as priests could carry with it the danger that distinctive diaconal ministry will be lost once again in the Church of England. More significantly, if handled creatively, the ordination of women as priests could promote the opportunity for men, especially ordained men, to rediscover their own liturgical diaconal ministry. In churches with more than one ordained member of the congregation it should become as common to see a woman presiding with a male deacon on her right, as a man presiding with a woman deacon on his right.

In very many churches, however, such a team of ordained people does not and will not exist. Here, one man or one woman normally exercises priestly liturgical ministry. In the case of a woman priest being the regular president of the eucharist, several aspects of eucharistic worship may be brought into fresh focus for worshippers.

The question of inclusive language has in part been brought into prominence in the Church of England since the late 1970s because of the experience of increasing numbers of women licensed to conduct public worship. Many of these women and their congregations found the exclusive language of the Alternative Service Book inappropriate and absurd. As congregations become accustomed to women priests praying the third eucharistic prayer of the ASB aloud, many will ponder the use of the phrase '. . . for all men' after the acclamations. The omission of the word 'men' is sanctioned in *Making Women Visible* and its use may well gradually die out. The same may also prove to be true of some of the post-communion sentences and other instances of exclusive language in the ASB.

The metaphors used to describe and address God in the ASB are almost exclusively male. The male dominance of the language of prayer is already the subject of much heated debate. The presence of women priests using these prayers may focus the debate more sharply, but it is unlikely to engender much immediate change in itself. This task will take time. The rather restricted contexts in which women priests currently work have already been mentioned, and are factors at work here. Nonetheless, exciting new liturgical writing by such authors as Janet Morley and Jim Cotter speaks of a fresh theological inclusivity, of women and men, black and white, young and old, gay and straight, and all grounded in an inclusive doctrine of God. The ordination of women to the priesthood raises questions and offers insights into the very nature of God, the creator of gender who is beyond gender. This debate is a continuing one in Anglican churches throughout the Anglican Communion which ordain women as priests. Anglican liturgical material from New Zealand, Canada and the United States of America is freely available in England, and may also serve to prompt liturgists official and unofficial to develop the ways in which public prayer is shaped in the Church of England.

This may appear to be rather mixed news to some people who have longed for the ordination of women as priests to promote immediately the inclusivity of liturgy and the declericalization of the priesthood. Views on whether or how these ends might be achieved vary hugely among ordained women and the congregations whom they serve. The experience of women priests in Anglican churches in New Zealand, Australia, the United States of America and Canada, culturally the societies most akin to that in England, suggests that the ordination of women as priests does not have any significant declericalizing effect upon received liturgical practice. Where male priests once presided exclusively, women priests may now preside exclusively. There is some anecdotal evidence that women priests are generally encouraging of lay ministries in liturgical worship as well as in other areas of church life, but firm evidence of this is not yet available. It could equally be said that some male priests are very encouraging of lay ministries. Research in the area of the processes male and female priests adopt to encourage and enable lay ministries would be very valuable at present.

What is much more evident is that in churches regularly served by one or more women priests, congregations are finding themselves rethinking their attitudes towards the involvement of children in worship, and towards the relationships between men and women in church leadership and beyond.

The question of children's involvement in worship is not one to be raised in a stereotypical fashion: the advent of a woman priest does not mean that children are bound to follow! Moreover, many male priests have excellent relations with children and are warmly encouraging of them in the worshipping life of the church. Nonetheless, the experience of women deacons with children suggests that on the whole ordained women are quite at ease welcoming children as regular worshipping members of a congregation. In part, this may be a carry-over from the home; the woman presiding over worship is used to relating to children and adults simultaneously. In part, some congregations have shared with their deacon the joys and trials of pregnancy and the birth of a child. The pregnant deacon or priest is no longer quite the shocking prospect that she may have seemed twenty years ago. Certainly the sight of a pregnant minister at the lectern or altar has and will focus in fresh and creative ways for some church members questions about the meaning of the incarnation.

The second main area of visual impact which the ordination of women as priests brings to the Church is that concerning the relationship between men and women under God. The ordination of women as deacons in the Church of England in 1987 carried with it its own inner paradoxes. Women became much more consistently liturgically prominent as deacons, but in the role of what has often been seen as the assistant to the priest. Not only are women in the home often responsible for laying the table and washing up, they have been equally so at the altar in the church. As those who now preside at the eucharist, women might be seen to be taking this role one step further. Now they are to be seen and heard preparing the food for the eucharistic meal, and acting as hosts at the meal itself. Crucially, the priest is she who presides, who takes the initiative in giving thanks at the meal. She is the one who acts with and for the people of God. She is not aping a man in so doing. She fulfils these functions and her calling in her own distinctive style. Put a man and a woman together at the altar, as priest and deacon, priest and server, and a creative dynamic with common human stereotypes of male and female roles is set up. This can provide a significant opportunity to discover in fresh ways what a theology of gender complementarity means if we are willing to receive it.

*

Ten years from now what might the liturgical life of the Church of England look like?

On the one hand, there could be little change. Congregations meeting for worship, using familiar rites, and presided over by priests at the eucharist; and priests, deacons or authorized lay people at other services. Whether the priest is male or female, the eucharist would be virtually unchanged; only the voice of the president would betray their gender. The language of worship would continue in its familiar forms, ASB style for some services, Book of Common Prayer for others. Debates about inclusive language would abate, lost within the need for stability come what may. The need for any theology of gender, and of gender complementarity within the ordained ministry of the Church, would be diminished. The women ordained priest would simply be absorbed into the received fabric of ecclesiastical practice.

On the other hand, the Church could learn from its experience of ordaining women to the priesthood. Congregations would meet for worship, using familiar rites, and presided over by priests at the eucharist, but with continuing and imaginative lay involvement in planning and shaping the worship. Episcopally authorized people, lay or ordained, would preside over other services. There would have developed some distinctive styles of celebrating the eucharist, shaped and informed by the experience of women as well as men who are ordained priest. The language of worship would be inclusive of male and female, young and old, gay and straight, black and white. Liturgical writing and action which celebrates the diversity of God's relationship with creation and humanity would be encouraged and used. There would be a rediscovery of the rich scriptural traditions of naming God in a variety of ways. Theologies of gender would be explored and discussed. Ten years on, women and men, lay and ordained, may together be discovering more of what it means to be caught up into the worship of the God who longs to make all things whole in Christ.

Reference

Liturgical Commission of the Church of England, *Making Women Visible: Inclusive Language for Use with the Alternative Service Book* (London: Church House Publishing, 1989).

IO

Hope fulfilled: hopes for the future

UNA KROLL

Introduction

Some years ago I moved from England to a small Welsh border town. I am a nun attached to an Anglican community: I live alone in a small house close to an Anglican church. I spend a good deal of time in prayer and silence: I am able to offer hospitality to visitors who want to enjoy some time in a quiet and peaceful house. I serve as a deacon of the parish church on a time-limited basis.

Around Easter 1994 some women friends, some of them living and working only a few miles away from here, were ordained to the priesthood of the Church of England. The Church in Wales, to which I now belong, has not yet decided to ordain women to the priesthood so I have watched these ordinations from a distance. I have seen the fulfilment of a life-long hope so I feel great joy, yet confess to some personal sadness that I cannot myself be ordained.

For the last 40 years I have been involved in all kinds of initiatives to bring about the ordination of women to the priesthood of the Church of England. Watching the struggle over this particular development in the life of the Church has been rather like watching a long labour, where, from time to time, things have gone badly wrong and both mother and unborn child have nearly perished. Thankfully, that phase is now safely passed and the 'child' has been born alive and well. However, the 'child' remains extremely vulnerable and could still be stifled now at its birth, or in the coming months, without too much difficulty unless a fairly large number of people agree to act as cherishing 'parents' who will nurture and protect the new life that has been created.

The main purpose of this chapter, therefore, is to encourage myself and others to reflect on the positive results that will follow from the ordination of women to the priesthood in the Church of England. I also want to see how we can cherish women priests and help them to develop creative ministries that will strengthen the life of the Christian Church. I will then point to some practical ways by which those of us who are not ordained can support and work with ordained women to ensure that this new life can grow and develop into maturity.

Women priests as symbols of God's activity in the world

Some of my feminist friends consider the doctrines and structures of the Christianity to be so permeated with patriarchy as to be irredeemable. I do not share that view. I am full of hope for the future. From where I stand, these initial ordinations are not simply a matter of people fulfilling their personal vocations: they are a transforming event in the life of the Christian Church and in society as a whole. When the mother of the Anglican Church, the Church of England, followed many of her daughter churches and took the momentous step of crossing this particular boundary line, her action had a significance that went beyond that of a mere decision of a province of the Anglican Church.

Some personal history will help to set in context my reflections. In 1972 I was a deaconess of the Church of England. In that year I attended an international conference of women ministers in New York. On the second morning an American Methodist woman minister presided at the Eucharist. I had never previously attended any worship service where a woman was presiding. Watching this woman as she stood alone at the altar I knew I had a choice: I could either heed my conditioned internal protest at the impossibility of such a Eucharist being valid at all and depart forthwith, or I could stay and receive Holy Communion and then see what I could make of such a shocking contradiction to my own tradition. I stayed. The effect on me of doing so was profound.

Shortly after the service had concluded, and we had started the next conference session, I noticed that I felt taller. Seeing a woman standing at the altar had made me feel more positive about my own goodness as a woman. To my astonishment I also realized that I had completely accepted the validity of the Methodist Eucharist. Within the space of half an hour I had been transformed from a narrow-minded, pious and loyal Anglo-Catholic traditionalist, who was secretly ashamed of being a woman, into someone who was happy and proud to be a woman. Moreover, I had discovered that I could receive God's grace coming to me through someone from another tradition. This was a change comparable to that which came over Peter when he fell into a trance on a roof top in Joppa and was told by God to receive as clean that which he had previously always thought of as unclean, a vision which subsequently led to him and others receiving Gentiles into the early Christian Church. For me that change of attitude was life-giving, though not immediately dramatic in its effects.

During the next two and a half years I had no further opportunity of attending any worship services presided over by ordained women, but it was during those years that I became a Christian feminist, in the sense of loving my own and other women's personhood, and I began to work for the recognition of women's goodness and worth in Church and society.

By 1974 there were Anglican women priests in Hong Kong, Canada and the United States of America, although their ministries were not officially acceptable in my own country. Nevertheless, from that time onwards I have taken every opportunity I could to participate in their ministry.

Now, after more than twenty years' experience of seeing women preside at the Eucharist and receiving the sacraments of reconciliation and Holy Communion from them together with their blessing, what can I say about the effects of that kind of experience? I, who formerly was damaged by my internal contempt for my womanhood, an attitude which also led to my distrusting other women, am now healed by God from that negative view. My steadily increasing trust of other women has also changed my attitude towards men. I no longer find myself denigrating them in subtle ways, something which I had done previously. Having to be dependent on men and perpetually subordinate to them was something I had disliked.

What has happened to one person can happen to others. Other women besides myself may feel taller because they see a woman preside at a celebration of the Eucharist. Other women can be healed from their distrust of their own kind. Other women may be liberated from their negative attitudes towards the men on whom they were formerly dependent for the sacraments. Some women will now feel they can offer gifts to the Church knowing that it will be possible to have them fully used in the service of God. It may not be so dramatic for them as it was for me, for these changes occur at subliminal levels in our collective human consciousness, but it is already happening and will go on happening as more and more people experience the ministry of women, ordained and lay, or see them about their pastoral work. It is not so much what women priests are now able to do that matters: rather, it is the symbolic fact of their being recognized as able to reflect and mediate God that is of primary importance. That is what will make a difference to the Church's mission to the world.

The social consequences of this symbolism will also be profound. There are various ways of looking at gender differences. One way has to do with women's ability to bear children and men's reactions to the fact that they cannot physically give birth. Hitherto, whether or not they are physical mothers, women have held in their collective unconscious the notion that the biological differences between women and men mean that men should somehow be compensated for their inability to bear children. Women have colluded with allowing biological differences to be reflected in their roles in society and in the Church, and have allowed themselves to be debarred from certain powerfully symbolic functions as a means of compensating men for their incapacity to give birth. The negative effect of this model in the lives of women may be seen in a tendency to seek subtle forms of power, without bearing full responsibility or accountability for their actions. This can be a way of seeking to compensate for their vulnerability during childbirth and the early months of parenthood. Now, however, in making their claim to exercise these symbolic functions, women reveal the truth that men and women are partners in parenthood not rivals. Thus the equal creativity of man's procreative acts may be seen to be restored to him as a direct result of the female priestly sign.

Men too will find their attitudes changing almost without their knowing it, and in a relatively painless way. The notion that has been present in some male clergy, that they are able to compensate for their inability to be physical mothers by doing some things that women cannot do, will gradually disappear. Subliminal jealousy about women's wombs will begin to fade and with it the distorting tendency to put women on a pedestal or to treat them as whores. At a symbolic level in human society, the primal enmity between men and women, recognized in Genesis 3.15, is being healed and they are being reconciled through Christ's work in and for them.

It is true that changes in law cannot by themselves alter people's attitudes. Some women and men will continue to hold to their sincere beliefs that the ordination of women to the priesthood is impossible or inexpedient. I respect those views though I do not share them. The number of women likely to be ordained is small enough to enable conscientious objectors to avoid meeting them and I do not know any woman who would wish to force her ministry on anyone who did not want to receive it. Nevertheless I believe that it is the freedom to choose to receive the ministry of women priests that now exists which will be instrumental in the acceleration of changes in attitudes towards women that are already occurring in Church and society alike.

The effects of these structural changes are already making themselves felt, for example, in the realm of prayer. This is where I personally feel the benefit of the decision to accept women into the ordained ministries of Churches. As a contemplative nun I am here to pray. I am here to be one of the spaces where Christ does his healing work of reconciliation. Nuns, like everyone else, are called to pay attention to some issues more than to others. Their calling to live lives of prayer means that God uses their aptitudes and particular gifts in quite specific ways. One nun, for instance, may feel called to offer her life for South Africa. Another will have a deep interest in the welfare of all children.

Another may adopt AIDS patients as her special area of intercession.

Up until now my own God-given personal vocation has been to pray for people on both sides of this conflict. On 11 November 1992 that question was settled at an institutional level by the General Synod of the Church of England, but I experienced no lightening of the sense of conflict during times of prayer. Indeed, for a time that burden was even heavier than before the decision was made. However, almost a year later, at the very moment when the voting figures from Parliament were announced, I realized that a weight had been lifted. It was not that there was a kind of victory dance going on inside my head. Not at all, for I shall continue to pray for women and men of sincere conscience who cannot accept the Church of England's decision, as I shall for the women who will be ordained to the priesthood. No! What had happened was that at that moment I had become conscious that a structural healing of a distortion in the relationships between men and women in the Church of England had taken place, and that this structural healing within the Church was experienced as healing in my innermost self. The distorting conflict that had gone on for so many years between Christians of differing opinions in the Church of England, and which had been experienced within me as conflict and load, had now been taken away.

While it is true that the burden of distorting conflict has been lifted, it is also true that the pain of my own frustrated vocation has increased. As a contemplative nun living alone in the heart of a small town I am visited by many people. I hear all kinds of true stories, some of which reveal the intense suffering of women who might have been ordained but for their age, local hostility or membership of a family, group or community that doesn't understand their particular vocation. Their frustration and pain resonate with my own. So that collective pain has to find its expression in prayer.

Such prayer often feels like anger: on behalf, perhaps, of an older woman who has served the Church faithfully over many years, yet is now deemed too old to be ordained; or of a married woman who cannot move from a parish which has used her talents for years, but which now finds it impossible to accept her as their priest. In prayer I can recognize my anger for them and I can take it to God. Over a period of years I have learnt not to suppress genuine feelings, especially unpleasant negative ones, but to allow them access into my conscious prayer without fear or shame. I also offer God my own yearning for priesthood. I trust that intercession and the acceptance of honest feelings of frustration will be taken up into the resurrection wounds of the risen, ascended and glorified Christ who acts in our world through the Holy Spirit. I believe that Christ can take every feeling that is human and transform it by his love so that it can be used in ways that go beyond our understanding.

This kind of prayer, real as it is, does not however take up all the energy that formerly went into the years of conflict. I now spend much time in prayer for other people in quite different situations. If the coming of women into the ordained priesthood of the Church of England will foster her mission by making more priests available for the service of Church and society, as I believe it will, it is also my belief that some of the energy of prayer among those who intercede, whether they be contemplative monks and nuns, ordained ministers or laity, will now be released for God's mission in different ways. I also believe that certain gifts in lay people will now be more available to the Church and society.

Having expressed my positive attitude towards the ordination of women at a symbolic level, the level of the collective unconscious, I also want to affirm my belief that women and men are significantly different in the way they tackle the same task, and I am eager to see women finding their own way of being priests in the Church of England rather than imitating the existing male models.

Women as persons with gifts from God that can be used by Church and society

It is immaterial to me whether the perceived and recorded differences between women and men are genetic in origin or environmental, or a mixture of both. For all practical purposes they are real: I can witness to that from personal experience, both from my work as a deacon of the Church in Wales and from my experience as a beneficiary of women's ministry.

So how shall we understand the particular gifts that we may expect to receive from women priests? When I ask for ministry from a woman priest, deacon or laywoman I expect to find in her, whether or not she has children, qualities that reflect the motherhood of God, the sisterhood of Christ and the close and warm friendship of the Holy Spirit, complemented, of course, by those less obvious qualities that reside below the surface, in her personality. These will reflect the fatherhood, brotherhood and friendship of the Holy Trinity. I have always had the option of going to male priests and have usually chosen those who are able to call on their motherliness as well as their fatherly qualities, but I have also recognized my need from time to time to go to a priest with a strong dominant streak in him, a characteristic that many people associate with male leadership. Formerly, however, I did not have the option of going to a woman priest at all, whatever her personality characteristics were. But the opportunity of having both options now is just as important for men. Were I to be a man I might want to go to a woman because I needed a mother/sister/girl friend/figure at that precise point in time, rather than a father/brother/man friend. It is a matter of freedom and choice. After all, God has created us to be male and female for a purpose, and I feel sure God wants us to be who we are.

My strong hope, therefore, is that women priests will not forsake their womanliness for the sake of conforming to an established male pattern of ordained ministry. My hope is that they will remain confident about being women, and not succumb to the temptation to dredge up so-called masculine qualities in order to conform to a pattern of ministry that may be alien to them. Of course, I would be the first to recognize that women vary a great deal in their personhood. I am also aware that society has done men and women a disservice by labelling certain personality traits as male and others as female, thus implying that a man who does not have supposedly male qualities is not a 'real man' and a woman who does not exhibit female qualities is not a 'real woman'. It is, I believe, only when you are confident in your 'persona', that part of you which you present to the world, that you can be comfortable with the deeper complementary qualities that undoubtedly exist in us all. The mature man or woman is the one who has integrated all aspects of his or her personality into consciousness. So, yes! I hope that women will be confident enough to bring to the service of the Church of England qualities and gifts that make full use of their genetic make-up as women. I believe that the fact that men and women inside and outside the Church will be able to choose freely to whom to go for help, advice, Word and sacrament, will enhance the Church's mission and hasten the coming of the Kingdom, and I want to illustrate how this has already happened in one rather specialized field of the Church's ministry.

Thankfully, all Christian Churches are now involved in caring for those who have been ill-used by men in childhood. These hurt people may consequently have great difficulty in relating to God as father, brother or lover. They sometimes also find it hard to entrust themselves to male priests. My own experiences as a child made it very difficult for me to relate to Christ through the mediation of the male priests whom I encountered in the Church of England when I first became a Christian disciple. It took me twenty years to realize that God loved me as a woman, indwelt me and wanted to use my gifts. During that time I met other hurt people like myself. So, under the guidance, I believe, of the Holy Spirit, we shared our pain, often with great difficulty. In those years of struggle we saw each other change and become able to find the honesty that enabled us to recognize the damage that *some* men had done to us without transferring our hurt feeling to *all* men. As far as I was concerned I do not think I would have been able to do that work without the skilled help of two women priests who were there when I needed them. It was only after receiving their help that I found myself able to entrust myself to male priests.

This kind of specialized ministry within the wider Christian ministry of the Church is skilled work, demanding considerable courage and patience from both the clients who have been hurt and from the companions who accompany them on the journey from a living death to resurrection life. We will need the gifts of Christian women in these areas of the healing work of the Church for a very long time, and it is so good to think that now these hurt people will be able to receive the sacraments of the Eucharist and of reconciliation from women as well as from men. I know that those who have been hurt by women in childhood experience similar difficulties in reverse. They need men to help them before they can entrust themselves to women. My point is that in this area of ministry we need all the help we can get from men and women who are ordained priests, able to mediate God's forgiveness to those who find it so difficult to forgive.

In other fields of work, experience shows that the ministry of ordained women is well received by those outside the Church. For the most part, they do not worry about the sex of the minister so long as they know their task and carry it out well. In those areas of parish ministry that touch the occasional church-goer, such as baptisms, weddings and funerals, in extra-parochial ministries such as chaplaincies in hospitals, hospices and universities, and in specialized ministries, such as the one I have outlined above, women are widely acceptable, and I expect to see much good come of the work that will now come to them because they are priests.

Helping women priests to find the support they will need if they are to be true to themselves

The Church of England's decision to ordain women to the priesthood has conferred respectability on opinions and practices that formerly could have been thought of as the somewhat adolescent rebellions or slightly eccentric unilateral declarations of independence by other younger provinces of the Anglican Communion. Gradually as women in England take their place at the altar their presence and symbolic roles will be assimilated into the collective unconscious of the English-speaking world. The implementation of the decision will undoubtedly affect relationships with other Churches, both Protestant and Roman Catholic, some will feel adversely, others advantageously. Either way, the Church of England's action will not have had a neutral effect. There will be change, certainly at a subliminal level where great developments are both initiated and consolidated. There will come a time when the collaboration of women and men in the ordained ministries of all Churches will be seen to be normative, but that time is not yet, and, for that reason, people who care about the life and mission of the Christian Church will have to be especially watchful and supportive to women priests for at least two or three decades to come, maybe for as long as half a century.

It is in the realm of the Anglican churches' congregational life that I see the most difficulties ahead, for both the supporters of women priests and for their opponents. We who belong to episcopal churches tend to have conservative tastes. We enjoy the pomp and circumstance of well-arranged ritual and ceremony. We are used to seeing men walking in processions, taking a leading part in worship and generally assuming control in important matters that concern the Church and its government. Although there are now many women who successfully do much the same work as men, they still lack experience and so are vulnerable to criticism. The first women priests will inevitably be a target for criticism. What they wear, how they walk, how they preach, how they conduct services will all be scrutinized and pigeon-holed. Many of them will suddenly find themselves in positions where they carry considerable responsibility for which they have had relatively little training. Some will live up to expectations, but at a considerable cost: some will crumble under the weight of having to carry the banner for *all* women. Others will become painfully aware that they are expected to fit into role stereotypes, and that the only way for them to feel comfortable will be to conform. Conform they will, but again at the cost of developing their own style of ministry. It would be sad, indeed, if a large number of women lived up to some people's expectations that they become dominant, 'bossy' people as soon as they become priests. It would be equally sad if some talented women tried to remain inconspicuous parish workers, as some people appear to be hoping they will. It will be the task of those of us who care about women priests to give them support so that the number who do crumble or conform to male models of priesthood, or underuse their talents, will be relatively small.

If women priests are to become generally acceptable to the Church of England, indeed to the whole Church of God, and if we, the people of God, are to make effective use of their gifts, then we will need to help them to be themselves rather than to try to gain acceptance by pretending to be honorary men.

Although some women may be fully accepted at once and so be able to be themselves, the general response to the presence of women in the ranks of the clergy is unfortunately likely to be patchy. Some will be relegated to subordinate positions; others will be given tasks that men don't want. Some will become seduced by flattery and think themselves more powerful and good than they are in reality; others may only gain their own power base at the expense of other women. It would be a particular tragedy if women priests became clericalized and distanced from lay people, if they abandoned a collaborative style of ministry for the sake of a little more power which they might gain if they collude with the status quo as it is found in a hierarchically organized ecclesiastical bureaucracy. Mercifully, however, there are signs that many people's vision of the role of ordained people in the Church is changing rapidly. Many more men now see their ministry as an enabling ministry. They see their role as ordained people as being given to them to encourage the gifts of the whole people of God to be used; they are more than willing to engage in collaborative styles of leadership. This kind of role can be seen as 'natural' to women and so they are likely to find themselves more at home in today's Church than they would have been 45 years ago when I became a Christian.

The Church of England has decided to ordain women to the priesthood, but men and women who openly dislike the idea can infect those with subconscious dislike and stir them up into open opposition through adverse criticism of the inevitable mistakes that the pioneers will make. The stakes remain high: a determined minority of people in opposition can still detract from the value that I and so many other people want to affirm when we support women priests.

There is, therefore, a compelling need to encourage and support ordained women, and I have been asking myself how this can be done in practical ways. The first way is through prayer. I cannot pretend to understand exactly how prayer works. I believe that prayer is a relationship initiated by God and that when I am quite still and empty I can sometimes become aware of God's love that is always there whether I recognize it or not. Prayer helps me to become aware of the mind of God for myself and for others. By being as open as possible to God's love, I become part of what God is being and doing now. I also think that the energy of my love can be used by God to support and sustain other people with less time to attend to prayer, and so I believe that those of us who care about the ministry of women need to go on praying and offering our energy to God to be used according to God's good pleasure.

Prayer frequently issues in action and I think people who pray often get strong intuitions as to what they are to do in the way of good works. This may involve offering friendship and a listening ear to a newly ordained woman, or to someone much more experienced but who still needs affirmation and encouragement. That is what I feel is important at an individual level, but I also think we need to make that kind of support visible at a collective level by encouraging women priests and their supporters to come together from time to time for worship, prayer for each other, and discussion. Initially there will be very few women in any one deanery, and some women may get very isolated, possibly even disheartened, so it may be better to organize such meetings at diocesan level.

In the past I used to find myself thinking that the hierarchy of the Church of England was insensitive in the way it deployed its women employees. They sometimes put women into impossible situations and then used the inevitable consequences to prove that they were unsuitable for leadership. For instance, deaconesses would be given relatively little leadership training in their student days. Then they would be sent into parishes where they knew their priest would take ultimate responsibility. When the Church began to take women's ministry more seriously, some of these women, who were by now middle-aged, were suddenly, and without any further training, given considerable responsibility. Some women managed to adapt. Others found themselves unable to handle the added burdens of decision-making. I listened to some of these women as they came to the point where they decided to resign. Some had received very little help and understanding from the more experienced male colleagues in their areas. That kind of thing is less likely to happen now that women and men are trained together, but it remains true to say that the expectations of unsympathetic fellow clergy and congregations can still wreak havoc. This will happen if they are insensitive to the particular difficulties of single women in charge of a parish or of married women trying to combine good parenting with an active parochial ministry or, for that matter, of husbands and wives sharing one stipend.

The first women priests will be pioneers. They will need support. Single men tend to attract practical support from the women of the parish, because even today they are not expected to be able to fend for themselves. Single women often find that they have to cope with a busy parish and with all their own domestic chores without much support. Observation suggests that most young male curates are sexually attractive and, if they want to, are able to find themselves partners relatively easily. Women curates do not appear to have as easy a time finding partners. Perhaps some careful research will uncover the reasons for this. Meantime, women ministers may find themselves very lonely since, initially at any rate, there will be some hesitation in offering help where it might not be wanted, and natural allies in the shape of other women ministers may be few and far between. They may benefit from quiet and sensitive help unobtrusively offered by parishioners. This might sound sentimental or self-evident, but it is surprising how many women struggle because people are too shy to offer them friendship and practical help. In my present situation I have received much practical and spiritual support and I can testify to how much difference it makes to the quality of one's life and ministry.

Married women have needs too: they have to organize their lives very carefully. Although they are sometimes emotionally better off than single women because they have partners, many do find that they are delighted if someone a little less close to them can, for instance, offer to do time-consuming practical jobs so as to relieve them of extra strain, or enable them to have some quality time with their family. It is necessary to be sensitive and discreet with one's offers, but it is, perhaps, better to offer and be refused than not to offer and miss a valuable opportunity which might make all the difference between 'burn out' and a fruitful ministry.

Both married and single women are still more often closely involved in caring for elderly or sick parents and relatives than their male counterparts and this fact of life will also add to the strains of ministry. That does not mean they should not be priests. It simply means that we as a Church need to be aware of the facts of twentieth-century life and take some responsibility for the way in which we care for our pastors.

Far from abandoning organizations such as the Movement for the Ordination of Women, which were set up to promote the cause of women's ordination and which have been so successful that it might seem logical to abandon them, we should reorganize them as foci for the support, encouragement and audit of women's ministry, both lay and ordained. It is, I think, important to retain at least one national organization which can circulate news in different regions. None of us should get complacent about our own area and neglect to give support and encouragement to women working under disadvantages elsewhere.

Initially some people may find the presence of a woman priest disturbing or even unpleasant. They too need help, not condemnation. They will have their own support groups but those who welcome the coming of women priests may be able to listen and offer prayerful and practical support to conscientious objectors, thus allowing them to distance themselves a little from the woman they find so difficult to accept. No one surely wants to force anyone to agree to what is truly unacceptable, and local support groups will want to do their very best to offer alternatives within the same parish to those who cannot attend church should a woman be standing at the altar. We are not called to compromise our principles: but we are called to tolerate each other's sincerely held differences, and to show each other consideration, compassion and love.

It will also be important to continue to enable discussions to take place between those who welcome the ordained ministry and those who do not, so that both sets of people can find their unity in Christ where everyone, whatever their shade of opinion, meets.

The way in which members of the Church of England behave towards each other during this next decade or two will matter. Women priests are now a fact of life. How we work through our differences and show the world that people can disagree without schism or rancour will matter greatly, perhaps even more than we realize, as we try to witness to the Gospel which we preach to the world.